prayers and so to sleep."

... and mumbled hurriedly a

... Soon I was in bed wrapped

... How glorious it was to see

... sky. How glorious to be

... to be alive. In the future

... I would do! The places to

... in the kitchen, broke in on my

... repeating with ... measure

... at my feet the angel Michael and

... Who exactly was the angel

... who was to find. Why was my

... him? So eternally sad?

... Surely it was foolish to

... night like this! Reading past

... were ———

... into sleep I heard

... voice in the next room.

... Michael and at my head the

THE
WORCESTER
ACCOUNT

S. N. BEHRMAN

THE

WORCESTER

ACCOUNT

Tatnuck Bookseller Press
335 Chandler St.
Worcester, MA 01602

Limited Edition Hardcover ISBN 0-9636277-8-3
Library of Congress Catalog Card Number 96-60111
Paperback ISBN 0-9636277-9-1
Library of Congress Catalog Card Number 96-61110

Book Design: Brady & Berg, Marianne Bergenholtz
Cover Design: Amorello Design, Janet Amorello
Photo Insert: RFD Communications, Ann Lindblad
Publisher: Lawrence Abramoff
Publishing Assistant: Jennifer Goguen
Printed in the U.S.A.

Limited Edition Hardcover endpapers: *a handwritten draft of "Malach Hamoves" by S.N. Behrman*
Paperback cover photo: *a 1913 photo from the collections of the Worcester Historical Museum*

The hardcover edition is a limited edition of 500 copies.

The following stories first appeared in the *New Yorker* Magazine and are published here by courtesy of the *New Yorker* Magazine, Inc.:

MALACH HAMOVES

MR. LAVIN, MR. LUPKIN, AND DR. ABERCROMBIE

THE IMPROVEMENT IN MR. GAYNOR'S TECHNIQUE

MY ROMANCE WITH ELEONORA SEARS

DEBS ON YOM KIPPUR

DAUGHTER OF THE RAMAZ

A LITTLE GLASS OF WARMTH

POINT OF THE NEEDLE

DOUBLE CHOCOLATE WITH EMMA AND SASHA

MR. WOLFSON'S STAINED-GLASS WINDOW

To order additional copies of this book, contact:
Tatnuck Bookseller Press
335 Chandler Street
Worcester, MA 01602-3402
FAX (508) 756-9425
phone (800) 642-6657 OR (508) 756-7644
INTERNET databooks@tatnuck.com

PREFACE

After more than fifteen years of searching for out-of-print copies of S. N. Behrman's *The Worcester Account* for customers, I finally found enough copies and read one myself. (The old tale of the shoemaker's kids going barefoot applies to booksellers as well.) *The Worcester Account* fascinated me immediately. I could imagine myself, my parents, and my grandparents in the stories. I saw my aunts, uncles, cousins, and neighbors. I revisited nostalgic pictures of my childhood, including the old synagogue where I attended services as a child. In addition to the Jewish immigrants Behrman describes, I saw immigrants of all nationalities—my Irish, Italian, Swedish, and French neighbors—who had journeyed to New York, Boston, and yes, even to Worcester, searching for a new and better life.

Sometime during my quest for this elusive book, I became a bookseller and publisher. After publishing several books about the history of Worcester, Massachusetts, publishing *The Worcester Account* seemed natural. My first stop was the Library of Congress. A search of their records turned up an address for Elza Behrman, the author's wife, in New York. Several unanswered letters later, I turned my attention elsewhere and opened Tatnuck Bookseller Marketplace, one of the largest independent bookstores in the country—but my interest in *The Worcester Account* never waned.

About two years after my initial attempts to contact Elza Behrman failed, my good friend and fellow publisher Tony King stopped in for a visit (and probably to buy a book, too). We chatted for a while about possible new publishing projects, when Tony mentioned *The Worcester Account*. I told him I thought I had reached a dead end. He mentioned that he knew someone's sister, who knew someone who was a relative of S. N. Behrman; but he couldn't quite remember the name. Tony left my office, but within hours he called me with the names Herb and Paul Cohan. I called Herb and found out that S. N. Behrman was the best man at his father's wedding. He liked my proposal to republish *The Worcester Account* and did his best to find a family contact for me. Herb called back a day or two later with helpful information from a cousin, Marian Behrman, about S.N.'s son, David

Behrman. To make a long story short, David was thrilled to participate in the republication of his father's work. He spent countless hours tracking down photographs for the book from his family and other sources. Without his kind help and patience, the photo section of this book would not have been possible. Many thanks to all who helped get this project off the ground and bring it to fruition.

I hope you enjoy *The Worcester Account* as much as I do. It's not just a "Worcester" book. It's the untold story of thousands of immigrant families seeking their fortunes in America. They came from all over the globe, many of them clinging desperately to the "old country" ways, to put down roots in America's fertile soil. *The Worcester Account* is their story—and yours and mine.

Lawrence Abramoff

TO KATHARINE WHITE

CONTENTS

1

A LITTLE GLASS OF WARMTH

On a grim and forbidding February day not long ago, at the end of a day's work, I lay down on the couch in my room to take a nap. It was late Saturday afternoon. My older brother had died a short time before, after a long and harrowing illness. Presently I was dreaming of him; there he was—alive, vital, casual. I cautioned myself against taking too seriously his seeming to be alive, because I knew that in dreams the dead often appear as the living, and I suspected that I was dreaming. However, the apparition of my brother persisted so naturally that I finally began to take sombre reassurance from what appeared to be the evidence of my senses. Gradually, I began to wonder why I had succumbed to the illusion, to the unfounded rumor, of my brother's death. There we were—both young and happy and living on Providence Street, in Worcester, Massachusetts. My brother was in Yale and he was wearing the cream-colored cap with a blue "Y" on the visor that he affected during his summer holidays. This sartorial detail, which I knew to be historically accurate, snapped for me the last clinging spider web of skepticism about his being alive. I then accepted the fact joyously, with immense relief and with a kind of defiant challenge to those unseen malevolent rumormongers who had spread about the false report of his death. I even repeated the rumor to my brother, and he laughed goodnaturedly and flexed his forearm as an assertion of life.

After that, it was all cozy. I saw him after a return from an afternoon's canoeing on Lake Quinsigamond. I heard him make a speech of acceptance when he was elected president of the Maccabees, a social club that had its headquarters next door to our tenement on Providence Street. It was the Fourth of July, and the Maccabees' yard was festooned with colored Japanese lanterns. I heard him say in conclusion, "And I shall fulfill this office to the best of my knowledge and ability." I had heard many such speeches and they all ended with this sentence, but there was a special inflection of confidence in my brother's voice and it made me proud of him. The evidence, the living evidence, that my brother was not dead but alive mounted and mounted, routing that unseen rogues' gallery of skeptics, of whose dissidence I was still dimly aware in some submargin of consciousness. It was a really lovely summer—a soft, eternal summer. Still, it merged into fall (further evidence that this was reality, not dream), and it came time for my brother to go back to New Haven. These departures were occasions. My brother was very popular, and all his crowd and a few small fry like myself used to go down to the old Union Station to see him off. We did so now, and the train came in from Boston, and my brother stood on the steps of one of the cars, laughing and talking and giving as good as he got in reply to the teasing jokes of those few among his friends who were Harvard men. (One could really not ask for more corroborative detail!) I was very happy, very proud, to have a brother who was doing well at Yale and who now promised to come back to Worcester and take me to the big football game when Yale played Holy Cross.

Then, suddenly, the halcyon moment was chilled and blighted with fear, for in the happy, laughing crowd wishing my brother Godspeed was *his* best friend and *my* best friend, Willie Lavin. This was dreadful. This destroyed everything. *For I knew that Willie was dead.* Willie was the best friend I have ever had, and his death many years ago was the greatest loss I had ever suffered. And yet there he was, laughing and joking and seeing my brother off

5

as he had done so many times when he was alive. The sight of Willie there paralyzed me. With the wild logic of dreams, I felt the whole structure of evidence supporting my belief that my brother had not died crumbling into dust. Another awful thing happened that was scarcely natural. The moment after I saw Willie, the train pulled out of the station, leaving my brother there, suspended in midair, unsupported by the car steps. Finding himself this way, his smile vanished. He looked bewildered suddenly—sad and anxious. I cried out to him. The sound of my voice roused me and broke off my dream.

I found that I had a terrible thirst, but I could not have been more than half awake, for I reached for one of the brass knobs that used to crown the iron posts at the head of the bed I slept in when I was a child. At the same time, my lips formed some words that bewildered me; they were familiar, but for the moment their meaning eluded me. The words were "I must have a little glass of warmth," and I kept repeating them. For a moment, lying there between sleep and waking, I thought that this strange phrase was something uttered by one of the phantoms in my dream, or something I had been saying to one of these phantoms while I was asleep. All the dream people had vanished; the only thing that remained was the vision of my brother's face, disembodied, suspended, and with an expression, already beginning to fade, that was tense and awkward, and anxious. I was similarly suspended, but between dream and reality, and I felt an agonizing pain of nonentity and a gasping reach for orientation in time and in space. The brass knob was not there. The objects in the room were unfamiliar, and I did not know whether it was still the Saturday afternoon when I had fallen asleep or whether I was waking up the following morning after sleeping through the night. Then I saw that I was dressed, so I knew it could not be morning. Everything was in recession and I was grasping vainly for a foothold on a nonexistent surface. The only reality was my painful thirst and the overwhelming wish to slake it with a little glass of warmth.

With agonizing difficulty, the fixed points in my present room were slowly recaptured, and I knew what had happened: I had lain down for a nap on a Saturday afternoon in New York City, far away from Providence Street and the Union Station, in Worcester. Still, when everything in the dream was gone and I knew that what had taken place in the station was now only the memory of a dream, my waking words persisted, in a kind of reiterated cadence—the whispered cry for "a little glass of warmth." For a long time I lay wondering about these odd words. And then in a flash I remembered exactly what they were, what they meant, and where they came from.

When I was a child, the Sabbath on the Hill, as we used to call the steep incline of Providence Street, was characterized by somnolent piety. It began at sundown on Friday and ended at sunset on Saturday. There were synagogue services Friday evening, Saturday morning, and early Saturday evening. Friday afternoons, my father used to take me to a public bathhouse which had a steam room, an attendant with a besom, and a tiny pool for lustral immersion—the symbol of the special cleansing required for the Sabbath day. The synagogue we attended was directly across the street from our flat, so it was especially convenient in inclement weather. These twenty-four hours theoretically, and in our house, as far as one could tell, even actually, belonged entirely to God. It was forbidden, for example, not only to touch money but to talk about it. It was forbidden to make a flame, so the gaslight fixtures had to be turned on early Friday evening, and enough coal put in the kitchen stove so that the fire would last till Saturday night. It was forbidden to carry bundles, to write a letter, to ride in any vehicle. When my pals on the Hill and I grew old enough to sniff emancipation, we used to walk boldly downtown to Main Street on Saturday mornings and ride up and down in the elevators of the Slater Building just for a fling at the illicit. Since the liftman demanded an objective before he would take us up, we learned to look up the names of the august Worcester law firms in the lobby directory, and arbitrarily we gave our business to one or another of them.

As I probed painfully for the origin of the long-lost phrase that I found myself repeating this particular Saturday afternoon, I thought of Saturdays in Worcester, and I suddenly recalled a scene that had taken place when I was very young—a snow scene. I couldn't have been more than six or seven, and it happened after the substantial Sabbath midday meal in our flat on Providence Street. As I look back on it, it was an oddity of our lives that in spite of the fact that we were very poor, there was always enough to eat. Though my father never, even by Providence Street standards, made a living, we always lived, and on the Sabbath our meals were always particularly good. To this day, I don't know exactly how it was managed. My oldest brother went to work very young, and I suppose the better-off relatives—especially my uncles—helped out from time to time. For a while, my father kept a small grocery store on Winter Street—it was his only business venture—and I imagine that during that time we ate the inventory. Perhaps this accounted for the early failure of the enterprise.

Thus, in my snow scene, my mother, her sister, and my grandmother sat in the kitchen near the stove after that good meal, gossiping—I hope piously. My grandmother lived with my aunt downstairs from us, and on Saturday afternoons my aunt would bring the old lady up for a visit. A rocking chair would be pulled into the kitchen for my grandmother, and she would be given the place of honor next to the stove. That day, my father was having his Sabbatical nap in the next room. Outside, a soft, silent, wet snow was falling; it had already gathered on the window sills, so that the lower parts of the panes were covered. Above were fir-tree configurations of frost, and on the inside of the panes a thin film of ice had formed, on which I was etching matching configurations with my thumbnail. The women spoke in low tones, because it was the Sabbath and in order not to wake my father; their voices made the murmur of a little stream running over pebbles, and there was a continuing sound from the stove, too—a kind of modulated, unhurried Sabbatical hum. The room was a little pocket of warmth, communion, and safety in a world of softly falling stars of snow. My improvisations on the frosty windowpanes grew in ingenuity and grace, and my thumbnail left a furrow of ice filings behind it, like the wake of a miniature snow-plow.

This peace was broken into harshly by a cry, with the quality of terror in it, from the next room. My grandmother went on rocking. "He's had a bad dream," she said placidly, out of her vast experience.

My mother rose at once and went automatically to the teakettle simmering on the stove.

The desperate appeal from the next room was repeated; the words were *"Ein glaesele warems!"*

By this time, my mother had poured a glassful of tea, and I followed her as she carried it into my father's room. My father was lying fully dressed on his bed. He was very dark in complexion and wore a full black beard; he looked, normally, like a benevolent Saracen, but that day, as he lay there on the bed, his face was grayish. His lips were muttering the Hebrew words that meant "Hear, O Israel, the Lord is our God, the Lord is one." This prayer, I was to learn later, was uttered in extremity, by the dying. My mother gave him the tea and he drank it greedily.

I became accustomed to hearing my father wake up from his Saturday-afternoon naps with a demand, sometimes casual and sometimes, as on this occasion, terrified, for *ein glaesele warems*. Later, I made my own literal translation of the Yiddish words—"a little glass of warmth." I even used to make fun of this strange expression, and repeated it, ridiculing it, to those of my playmates who were unfamiliar with it. We used, in parody, to invite each other in for ice-cream sodas at Elkind's with the elegant mock-ritual question "A little glass of cold?" This symbolized the aeons we had travelled beyond the comical rigmarole of our elders! We need not have been so contemptuous. The analogy so often made, especially in verse, between sleep and death is a false one; our little life is not round-ed with a sleep, since it must be a characteristic of death that it is dreamless. Sleep is not the death of each day's life; often it is a more vivid and distorted extension of it.

I echoed, on my own awakening that February afternoon so short a time ago, not only my father's words but his desperation. He must have been lost in the phantasmal jungles (reanimating what dead of his own?), and his cry for the little glass of warmth symbolized the desire of all of us to break off the winding filaments of the nightmares that bedevil us and find a foothold on the tiny, lit plateau, incessantly eroded by time, that is everyone's fragment of reality.

It was an early perplexity of mine that my father, a godly man, who believed completely in the immortality of the soul, should be so obsessed by the fear of death. He indulged in funerary fantasies (supported, he said, by ancient Hebrew texts) of the lacerating pains to which the body was subject after death. For him, evidently, the immortality of the soul was accompanied by a persistence of corporeal sensibility. I have heard quoted these words of an ancient sage: "Where life is, death is not; where death is, life is not." But this was not at all my father's idea. For him there was no such dichotomy. The security of his belief in immortality was threaded with lurid visions of continuing expiatory pains after death for the lapses of his lifetime; it was an immortality of guilt. There was nothing jolly or comforting in this concept, no hope of joyful reunion with lost loved ones, no atmosphere of club night. It was an immortality of loneliness, each soul with its personal account to settle, and no borrowing to tide one over.

As I grew older, the perplexities multiplied. I wondered how my father, living, as he did, under a canopy of faith as wide as eternity, could permit the constant obtrusion of petty civil war within our house. I wondered, too, how there could be quarrels within the portals of the house of God across the street. I never in the least understood the relationship between my father and my mother. My mother was quiet, my father darkly voluble. My mother's pietism was passive, my father's the active core of his life. My mother stood in worshipful awe of my father's book learning. She herself was not expected to know; it was taken for granted that she would be ignorant forever. Indeed, for her to be learned, or even knowledgeable, would have constituted a kind of solecism, a violation of good manners. Their relationship, as far as I could tell, was curiously impersonal. Both of them were tenderhearted and loving people, but there was never any manifestation of love between them; their tenderness was all lavished on their children. For my mother, it must have been like living with a priest of the Delphic mysteries to whom she could never

13

hope to be more than an acolyte. She was relegated, by common consent, to a comfortable and, I suspect, not uncozy darkness. They had been married before they emigrated to this country. But what was their life before then? How did they meet, how woo? (I asked them once, but the inquiry was considered frivolous.) I don't ever remember hearing my parents converse, and they never even chatted. My father would expound on law and ritual; my mother would listen. Most of the time my father was buried in his religious books, and my mother recognized it as her function to keep this communion undisturbed; she was like the wife of an artist who is engaged in creating a masterpiece and whose concentration she must incessantly strive to protect. And yet their relationship cannot have been as neutral as it appeared, because it was harshly broken into from time to time by fierce quarrels. I was never present at one of these quarrels, but I overheard them from another room. I cannot remember what they were about, but I remember their intensity. My mother would say very little; indeed, she would be almost completely silent except that she cried, softly. My father's voice would rise higher and higher in uncontrollable fury, and then there would be a tinkling crash as a glass or a cup shivered on the table—at the point, evidently, where his vocabulary proved inadequate to his grievance. Such quarrels were infrequent but shattering; for days after one of them, my mother would be sad as well as silent, and my father, when he returned to his studies, which he always did immediately, would have a smoldering look as he bent over his books, as if he were churned up still with resentment at the untoward interruption, caused by some fallibility in my mother, of his toiling search for salvation.

These quarrels, rare though they were, caused me intense pain. They were also confusing. I wondered how my father, so patently occupied with the eternal, could permit himself to be so roiled by the temporal. I once spoke to my mother about this, a week or so after one of these outbursts. My mother was defensive, and, as usual, laconic. "Your father," she said simply, "is a *kaissen*"—a fierce-tempered man. She let it go at that; she would have considered it unreasonable to expect a *kaissen* to coo like a dove when he was irritated.

The *coup d'état* at the Providence Street Synagogue was even more bewildering than the quarrels at home. It concerned the inauguration of a new rabbi, who had been duly elected and whose name was Silver. From the start, the proposal of Rabbi Silver for this post was the cause of a bitter feud among the members of the congregation. The dissenting faction was headed by my Uncle Harry. He was my mother's brother, and his devotion to my father, whose learning he revered, amounted to worship. He was himself unlearned, but he knew erudition when he met it. Some time before this, my Uncle Harry had made a tremendous short cut to a vast sea of learning when he married Ida, the daughter of the Ramaz, who was a world-famous rabbi. One of the first things Harry did after he achieved this fabulous coup was to arrange a meeting between the Ramaz and my father. After he had introduced the two men, he left them alone in his flat, modestly aware of his unworthiness to be present at a communion between two such cognoscenti. I remember hearing my older brothers tell of Uncle Harry's glowing, breathless entrance into our flat to report on the results of the meeting. A big, blond man, he was perspiring with triumph. "The Ramaz says your father is a *kenner* [a learned man]," he blurted out ecstatically, as if he were announcing a Nobel Prize. Moreover, Harry was manifestly relieved at having his own opinion of my father, which had been based on instinct rather than scholarship, confirmed by an authority that was unimpeachable.

Uncle Harry's bitterness against Rabbi Silver was due to the simple fact that the Rabbi, within Harry's hearing, had made a slighting remark about my father, casting doubt on his eminence as a Talmudist. Perhaps Rabbi Silver, humanly enough, slightly resented my father's reputation on the Hill, and felt that it encroached unduly on his own domain. But my Uncle Harry was no mean *kaissen* on his own account, and when he heard this disparaging remark he saw red. He made a solemn vow. "You will never become Rabbi of the Providence Street Synagogue," he told the candidate. Nevertheless, Rabbi Silver was elected. Uncle Harry defied the democratic process. When the day came for Rabbi Silver to be inducted, Harry, with a loyal cohort of adherents, forcibly barred his entrance into the synagogue. The rebel squad was compactly organized, and the Silver men retired, taking the new Rabbi with them. Uncle Harry repeated his vow that Rabbi Silver would never enter the synagogue. This impossible situation was resolved by my father, who persuaded Uncle Harry to withdraw his opposition. He realized that Harry's personal honor was involved; with a certain humor, he pointed out to Harry that since he (my father) had been given a *kosher tzettl*, or certificate of purity, by the great Ramaz, Harry could afford to ignore the cavillings of lesser lights. Harry saw the point and rested on his oars. Later, my father and Rabbi Silver became firm friends. But the feud was a whirlpool while it lasted, and it increased my perplexity about the relations between man and God; to me they seemed needlessly edgy.

My father was extraordinarily sensitive to the feelings of other people and was constantly on guard against hurting them. This may have been the result of his own persecution complex, brought with him from Lithuania, where he had lived under the shadow of a blood feud reaching back into the dim corridors of time. He lived his entire life as if in ambush, perpetually under the shadow of ancestral massacre. All sensitiveness, at bottom, is an intimation of pain and of fear, for oneself or for others—a shrinking from the bruise, and an awareness of transitoriness. It was because of this delicacy of feeling in my father that his occasional outbursts at my mother shocked and bewildered me. They were out of character. I remember that once, in a gathering of some of his friends at our house, my father was greatly put out with my Uncle Harry, who boasted of the virtues and of the promise of his children to a man whose tragedy was that he was childless. After the man left, my father chided Uncle Harry for his thoughtlessness. My uncle understood and was contrite. Having made his point, my father then told Harry that his lapse was human and natural. Thus restored to pride, Harry went on to explain to my father—who was *not* childless—how difficult it was to be secretive about children as remarkable as his own.

My father's small grocery store on Winter Street was a frail enterprise at best, and my planned and persistent thefts from its stock must have hastened its demise. What I stole were the little pictures of celebrities that came in the packs of Sweet Caporal cigarettes. I was shortsighted and had to wear glasses very early. The glasses were always getting broken, and each lens cost seventy-five cents to replace. It got to be an agony to me to report at home that I had again broken my glasses. Simultaneously, I discovered that complete sets of Sweet Caporal pictures had a market value; the more opulent among my pals on the Hill would pay cash for them. One day, in a crisis of guilt over breaking a lens that had been replaced only the week before, I desperately conceived the notion of stealing some of these cigarette pictures and selling them, so that I could get the repairs made myself and would not have to tell my father about the new disaster. It worked. I must have opened five dollars' worth of packs of cigarettes to get enough pictures for the seventy-five cents I needed. That was the first time; after that I took to filching the pictures out of general acquisitiveness. It was a simple operation, because Sweet Caps came in cardboard packs, which in turn were inserted into cardboard shells. I had only to slide a pack out of the shell, remove the work of art, and slide the pack back again. The excise stamps luckily did not seal the opening, as they now do, but were pasted on the back of the package. Every once in a while, my father would leave me to mind the store. One day he came back sooner than I had expected and caught me red-handed in this criminal activity. Before me on the counter were the raped packages,

19

and in my hand a halfdozen colored prints of famous contemporary prizefighters, wearing shorts and crouched in belligerent attitudes. I was terrified. I expected the worst. Greatly to my surprise, my father was sad rather than angry. He was so gentle that I felt awful; it would have been much better for me if he had lost his temper and got it over with. He questioned me and I told him about the broken glasses. He reproached me for not telling him; he would have managed to find the money to repair them. But how could he—or I—repair the sin of my having broken one of the Ten Commandments? The Ten Commandments were his personal code, and ever since I could remember, he had patiently expounded them to me. What failure was it in him that rendered his teaching so ineffectual? He was disconsolate.

Then his eyes fell on the pictures. "Who are these people?" he asked. This diversion of interest proved to be a stroke of luck for me. It was fortunate for me that the photographs were not, as they so easily might have been, of admirals or actors or generals. That I was collecting prizefighters added acutely to my father's unhappiness; it compounded the original sin, but at least it distracted him from that sin. The broken Commandment was forgotten, and he now attacked me for my choice of heroes; he set out to deracinate a mistaken ideal. I was so relieved to be fighting on more defensible ground that I expressed an enthusiasm for these giants that

I did not feel. My father got really excited; he saw that he had much work to do. Prizefighters! Only recently, in the Yiddish paper from New York, he had read that a prizefighter had died from injuries received in the ring. My father had shifted his ground from "Thou shalt not steal" to "Thou shalt not kill." These mercenaries, he said, shoving aside the pictures with loathing, kill for money. Killing and mutilation were in their hearts as well as in the hearts of the spectators. I gathered that my father would have forgiven me on the spot had these little pictures been of men of good will—of Spinoza, say, and the Rambam. (Rambam was the affectionate nickname for Maimonides, based on the ancient doctor's initials.) But the Sweet Caporal people had not—up to then, at least—hit on the idea of using my father's cherished worthies as subjects for their come-ons, and I was stuck with Jack Johnson and Joe Choynski. My feeble defense of these wonderful physical specimens deepened my father's wrath. He warmed to his theme; he invoked, as was inevitable, our slaughtered ancestors—his and mine. How could I, whose forebears had suffered so from violence, honor as heroes those who made a profession of violence? Would I, he shouted at me, condone murder? On this point I would not commit myself; by my silence I allowed him to think that I might. I preferred being accused of a crime I had not committed to standing sentence for the one I had; I repeated my stupid defense of Jack and Joe as practitioners of a manly art. From this point on, my father took me for a potential murderer and mobilized all his resources toward averting the dread actuality. He picked up one of the hated pictures and tapped it gingerly with his finger. "Thou shalt not kill," he adjured me solemnly. He was carried away, as if struck for the first time— and maybe he was—by the amazing revolutionary quality of the concept behind this prohibition, which had been enunciated first by one of *his* ancestors. (For the moment, he stopped sharing ancestors with me!) He expounded on what a remarkable feat of the imagination it was, and what courage it must have taken, to make such a heterodox pronouncement in a time when killing was accepted social behavior. Conscious of having had a very narrow escape, I promised faithfully to renounce murder and to forswear prizefighting forever. And, indeed, I have, as far as I know, kept these promises to my father. I have certainly, to this day, never seen a prizefight. On that critical morning, my father scotched whatever taste I might have developed for pugilism.

There were other feuds—contemporary as well as ancient ones—to add to my perplexities. One of these was of such searing intensity that the scars it left have not, after fifty years, entirely healed. I was astonished to learn not long ago that because I had confessed to having loving memories of a certain Providence Street girl, a very old friend of mine had expressed considerable bitterness; it had wounded him that I had apparently forgiven this girl for a crime that in my eyes she had certainly never committed. Providence Street youth, en masse, was in love with Myra Ellender—or so I shall call her— just as Oxford youth was with Zuleika Dobson, although there all resemblance ceased. Myra was a contemporary of the younger of my two older brothers, and he was in love with her, too.

Among the many suitors who came in quest of Myra were the two Eisner boys, Dan and Aaron, the eldest sons of a large and fairly prosperous Providence Street family. The younger, Aaron, was a poet; at least, he wrote verse. Aaron was inclined to be secretive about his poetic vocation; he would show his verses to no one except Myra, who adored them. Aaron's reticence about his poems dated from the time when an English teacher in the Classical High School wrote in the margin of one of them, in red pencil, "Fine feeling—conventional imagery." Like so many prone to art, Aaron ignored the compliment and brooded over the animadversion. Myra, to whom most of Aaron's poems were dedicated, did not find the imagery conventional; she thought it wonderful. "Aaron is a poet!" she would say flatly in defense of him, implying that this was more than sufficient compensation for his deficiencies as a dancer, sportsman, and general

23

good fellow. Aaron was dark, silent, withdrawn, and melancholy; Dan was redheaded, gay, vivacious, and very popular—that is, until Myra began to show a marked preference for him. Then his rivals began to discover the reverse side of his qualities, and they began to wonder whether his gaiety was not an indication of superficiality, and his goodfellowship somewhat artificial. Myra spent a great deal of time with Aaron; she was the confidante of all his dreams. She was in ecstasy over his poems and was flattered that they were dedicated to her. But when it came to the point, she chose Dan.

Aaron was not the only one to suffer because of her choice. Willie Lavin did, too. Of all my brothers' friends, Willie was the one my father esteemed most highly. Had Willie lived "at home," my father used to say, he would surely have become a *gaon*, or genius. By this he meant that if Willie had been born and brought up in the Lithuanian village his parents came from, he would naturally have devoted himself to theological studies and, because of the subtlety and inquisitiveness of his mind, become eminent in them. At the time, Willie was majoring in chemistry at the Worcester Polytechnic Institute and doing brilliantly in it. My father had no objection to chemistry; he thought it was all right as far as it went, but he resented its presumption in displacing what should be everyone's major preoccupation—to get a sure footing on the complicated and thorny approach to God. In spite of this, Willie and my father were great friends; they had prolonged discussions on abstract philosophical questions in the evenings in our kitchen, to which I listened from my bedroom next door.

One day, Willie brought to my father a dilemma that was not in the metaphysical realm at all but uncomfortably close to home. It concerned Myra, whose marriage to Dan Eisner was only a few weeks off. Willie, as well as my brother, had been in love with Myra. Both of them had chafed when Myra made her choice but had accepted the inevitable with what good grace they could muster. Now Willie felt that he had to impart to my father a devastating fact about Dan, which had been confided to him—in violation of professional ethics— by his friend Dr. Nightingale. Jim Nightingale was the family physician of most of us on Providence Street, and he and Willie had a special friendship, founded on the rock of science. A few evenings before, Willie had dropped into Jim's office for a chat about chemistry. The phone rang and Willie heard Jim talking to Dan, inquiring how he felt and asked him to come in in the morning. After Jim hung up, Willie asked him whether Dan had been ill. Jim said casually that Dan had diabetes and had not much more than two years to live. Willie was overcome. "How can that be when he is marrying Myra in a month?" he asked. "Marriage," said Jim jocularly, "is no cure for diabetes!" Jim seemed anxious to return to chemistry, but Willie was so appalled by the implications of Jim's prophecy that he could not drop the subject. "Shouldn't Myra be told?" he asked. "I told Dan he ought to tell her," said Jim, "but if he doesn't want to, that's his business. Don't worry about Myra. She'll be an attractive widow!"

Lying in my bed in the next room, supposedly asleep, I overheard Willie repeating this conversation to my father. When Willie had finished, there was a long silence. Finally, I heard Willie say—and his voice was somewhat tremulous—"Well, Reb Yosel, don't you think we ought to do something?" Still my father said nothing. Willie took the plunge. "Don't you think we ought to tell Myra?" he said.

There was another silence. At last my father spoke: "With what motive, my son?"

I had never heard my father address Willie in this way before. He usually addressed him by the affectionate nickname of "Velvel." Why, I wondered, does he now refer to him as his son when Willie is not his son?

There was no answer from Willie. I felt that my father's question had probed some delicate concealed membrane of emotion. After a moment, my father repeated the question. "With what motive, my son?"

Willie's voice, when he answered, had risen in pitch. "Don't you think we ought to do something to prevent such a tragedy?" he asked.

"Is Dr. Nightingale, then, omniscient?" said my father.

"He knows Dan has got diabetes," said Willie stubbornly. "He knows he'll be dead within two years."

"Can he peer into the future? Is he God? What if, in those two years, some specific is discovered that may cure Dan? What if, through divine intervention, he gets better? Look into your heart, my son. Is it to avert tragedy that you wish to tell Myra this or for some other, less disinterested reason?"

I began to apprehend, dimly, what my father meant. So did Willie. He defended himself stoutly. "Don't you think we ought to save her from early widowhood? A beautiful young girl . . ." His voice trailed off.

"In any case," said my father dryly, "she will not be a widow long. Is not Aaron in love with Myra? If this happens, Aaron will have the right to marry her. He *will* marry her, unless he and his family decide to give her a *halitzah*, which I very much doubt they will. You know this law, my son?"

Willie may have known, but I did not know. It was the first time I had ever heard that strange word. I have found out since that more than a hundred and fifty pages of my father's Talmud were devoted to the exposition of this law.

Meanwhile, my brother had come in from his nightly work in Willie's father's store. Apparently he had already heard from Willie the news about

Dan's health and now he barged head on into the argument. "It's true Willie and I are both interested in Myra," he said. "But that's not why we want to tell her. We want to tell her for her own sake. If, as you say, after Dan's death she'll have to marry Aaron, it's all the more reason to tell her. She doesn't like Aaron!"

"She has told me often she loves Aaron," said my father.

"Not that way," said my brother bluntly.

There was a silence, and I could imagine my father appraising both of them. "Look into your hearts," I heard him say finally. "Do not take on the prerogatives of God."

Evidently neither Willie nor my brother cared to look into their hearts at that particular moment.

"Let's go down the line for a soda," said Willie.

"Fine," said my brother, as if greatly relieved to have even a brief postponement of divine responsibility. I heard the door slam after them as they went out.

I lay for a long time trying to unravel the mystery of what I had overheard. Dan was to die. How could this be? I had seen him only a few days before on the Providence Street trolley and he had greeted me cheerfully. He had looked trim and natty. Dan was a careful dresser; his beautifully knotted tie bulged just enough between the margins of his high, stiff linen collar—the sort of collar often seen at that period in the color lithographs of

John Drew on the theatre posters announcing the actor's arrival at the Worcester Theatre. John Drew was generally acknowledged to be "the best-dressed man in America." How could one predict death so calmly in relation to a man dressed like that? Did Dan know? If he knew, how could he take so much trouble about knotting his tie? If he knew, if Dr. Nightingale had told him, why didn't he take measures against the dread invader, as I was doing even now? My hand reached instinctively for the brass knob at the top of the iron bedpost and closed compulsively around it—my usual childish gesture of clinging tightly to the terrestrial during my frequent night fantasies of the approach of death. From the kitchen, as I fell asleep, I heard the familiar drowsy creaking of the floor boards as my father paced the room intoning his nightly prayers: ". . . and may the Angel Michael be at my right hand; Gabriel on my left; before me, Uriel; behind me, Raphael; and over my head the divine presence of God."

In the second year of his marriage to Myra, Dan did die. It was before the discovery of insulin. Almost from the day of Dan's death, even we children became aware of a whorl of dispute between the two families—Dan's and Myra's. I have said that the virulence of this controversy was so scarifying that at least one of the participants was still exercised about it nearly a half century later and bore me a grudge for speaking warmly of Myra. I myself recalled it unexpectedly one night in Weld Hall, at Harvard, some fifteen years after Dan's death. I was enrolled in a writing course called English 12, which was taught by a famous Harvard figure, Charles Townsend Copeland. Copey, something of an eccentric, gave us only one assignment for homework—to read a chapter of the King James Version of the Bible every night before going to bed. He fondly hoped that this would help us form a style. For a time, at least, I conscientiously followed his instruction. One winter night, I was drowsily absorbing style from the Book of Ruth. Suddenly I sat up straight in bed, flicked by the whip of recognition. I was deep in the autumnal romance of Ruth and Boaz (the wealthy landowner who was a relative of Ruth's late husband), and had reached the point where Boaz finally knows his own mind and decides to marry Ruth. There is a quite intricate inheritance situation, involving the land of Elimelech (Ruth's dead father-in-law), which his widow, Naomi, had inherited, and there is a secondary story, involving an even nearer kinsman of Ruth's late husband than Boaz; this kinsman, apparently, is next in line both to redeem the property and to marry Ruth. But he is cagey. Boaz has decided that Ruth is the girl of his dreams. Absorbed in all this, I read:

Then said Boaz, What day thou buyest the field of the hand of Naomi, thou must buy it also of Ruth the Moabitess, the wife of the dead, to raise up the name of the dead upon his inheritance.

And the kinsman said, I cannot redeem it for myself, lest I mar mine own inheritance; redeem thou my right to thyself; for I cannot redeem it.

Now this was the manner in former time in Israel concerning redeeming and concerning changing, for to confirm all things; a man plucked off his shoe, and gave it to his neighbour: and this was a testimony in Israel.

Therefore the kinsman said unto Boaz, Buy it for thee. So he drew off his shoe.

The shoe stopped me; the shoe made me sit bolt upright in bed. Where, formerly, had I encountered this shoe? What was it about the shoe?

I read on:

Moreover Ruth the Moabitess, the wife of Mahlon, have I purchased to be my wife, to raise up the name of the dead upon his inheritance, that the name of the dead be not cut off from among his brethren, and from the gate of his place: ye are witnesses this day.

I forgot completely that I was reading for style. I felt intimately, though enigmatically, concerned. It was as if this ancient and bizarre romance were a contemporary mystery to which an essential clue was maddeningly eluding me. Hadn't I, some time long ago, overheard a conversation involving this very situation? Didn't I know—hadn't I heard—something about the ceremony of the shoe? Hadn't there been a terrible fight over it? And what was the fight about?

I couldn't stand it. I got up, put on my bathrobe, and went into the hall to put in a call to Willie, in Worcester. Willie knew all about it. Willie told me.

After Dan died, Aaron stepped forward to claim Myra. According to the ancient Jewish law, the widow of a son with a surviving brother cannot marry anyone but that brother unless she gets from the brother a *halitzah*, or release. One of the symbols in the ceremony is the removal of the brother's shoe by the widow, if her husband has died childless; by this gesture, the brother is released from the obligation of marrying her, and she becomes free to marry whomever she desires. (*"Halitzah"* means literally "taking off," "untying.") But in Myra's case, Willie told me, Aaron did not want to be released. He wanted terribly to marry Myra. She had always said she loved him and his poetry; to be sure, he was no longer a poet, having given up his versifying for the law, yet he had never wavered in his love. He could understand her having impulsively succumbed to his older brother's dash, but his brother was dead, and surely now Myra would marry him.

Myra wouldn't. She loved him as she always had; Aaron was very dear to her, but she would not marry him. Aaron's father, a choleric man—an uncontrollable *kaissen*, in fact—and the whole family were in an uproar. If Myra wouldn't marry Aaron, they would support him in refusing to give her a *halitzah*, which meant that, according to the Talmudic law, she couldn't marry anyone else. It was a terrible time, Willie said. The Eisners were, by Providence Street standards, a powerful family. Eisner *père* was a proud, arrogant man. He had an overdeveloped patriarchal sense, and of his seven children four were unfortunately daughters, who could not be expected to perpetuate his name. Aaron was his second son, and the third was only seven years old at the time of Dan's death. Frustrated in everything so far—in poetry and in love—Aaron became embittered by Myra's second refusal. He insisted on his rights. In the absence of a formal religious court, he came to see my father, who had a kind of quasi-judicial authority in the community as a learned man, and who was also a friend of his family, to ask him to persuade Myra to obey the letter of the Hebrew law.

Unexpectedly, my father pleaded with Aaron not to insist on his prerogative. He had talked to Myra, who wept and told him that although she adored Aaron—the manuscripts of his poems, she

said, were still her most cherished possessions—
she could not bring herself to marry him. My father
asked Aaron to disregard the letter of the law—to
be magnanimous. Aaron, melancholy and withdrawn, said nothing. He went home and told his
father, who flew into a towering rage against mine.
(It was the start of a feud between the two men that
was never healed in the lifetime of either, and smol-
ders, as I have indicated, even yet.)

Willie told me, too, that night, how he and my
brother had shamelessly encouraged Myra in her
recalcitrance. Myra's father was a religious man; he
shuddered at the thought of his daughter's defying
the law. But Myra held out. So did the Eisners. They
would not let Aaron give a *halitzah*, and thus they
condemned Myra to lifelong widowhood. For two
years, Myra lived on in this dreadful suspended
state, during which time she went out with Aaron,
my brother, and Willie. Then, suddenly, Myra did a
shattering thing—performed a feat of emancipation
compared to which Nora's exit from the doll's
house was a peaceful stroll in the country. She lightly threw over centuries of tradition, snipped the
Gordian knot of legal entanglement, and married a
lace salesman from Albany, leaving Willie and my
brother to console each other for the second time.

After my long telephone conversation with
Willie, I went back to my room and got back into
bed. But I couldn't, somehow, pick up with Ruth
where I had left off; she was still waiting there for

her kinsman to take his shoe off—just as Myra had waited, ten years before on Providence Street, and waited in vain. I reflected, though, on the bizarre histories of Ruth and Myra; Boaz had been so much luckier than Aaron. I thought with feeling of poor Aaron, sadly pleading his hopeless cause, and tried to reconstruct in my mind the scenes of his wooing, his interview with my father, and his inability, so bogged down was he in love, to take a high line. Oddly enough, Aaron died, too, several years after his rejection by Myra, and the patriarchal Eisner was unable to avert the fate that he dreaded most of all; he went to his grave with his name unperpetuated—in the words of the Book of Ruth, with the name of his dead "cut off from among his brethren, and from the gate of his place. . . . "

From that night in Weld Hall, in Cambridge, in 1915, to the February afternoon in 1953 when I lay down in my apartment in New York to take a nap, Aaron had disappeared for me among the anonymous dead. It remained for a nightmare to resurrect Aaron. Not even when I was told that his only surviving brother, my friend and contemporary, had been angered by a warm reference of mine to Myra in a quite different connection, did I really remember Aaron. He had been so sad and passive and ineffectual. His brother Dan, though, I always remembered vividly. Submerged memories of the dead are like actors waiting for a cue in the wings of the subconscious; the more assertive come on oftener. Even as a ghost, Aaron lacked vivacity and had to take second place to his livelier brother. Perhaps it would have been different had he not died without tasting, however briefly, what, in one way or another, we all reach for—a little glass of warmth.

2

PROVIDENCE STREET IN SUMMER

We lived, when I was a child and until I left Worcester, in a triple-decker tenement a quarter way up the long hill that was Providence Street. The street belonged to a few Irish, to a few Poles, and to us. The Messrs. Graton and Knight had occupied, when I was very young, two white houses at the opposite corners of Waverly and Providence Streets; these had been the residual islands of a lovely, tree-shaded New England street. Mr. Graton and Mr. Knight were the last of the "Yankees" who lived on the hill. (It seems strange to me now that my immigrant elders always referred to the native New Englanders as "Yankees," as if they themselves were Southern aristocrats!) As the

"Yankees," no longer able to afford the maintenance of their large places, moved away, an enterprising real-estate man bought up their properties and put up the triple-deckers.

These triple-deckers, which straggled up our hill, were mostly sadly in need of paint jobs and their mass appearance was somewhat depressing. But in many other respects they were not so bad. They had balconies, front and back, which we called piazzas. The yards in the back had fruit trees—cherry and pear and apple. We had more pear trees in our back yard at 31 Providence Street than Mr. Carnegie had in his at 91st and Fifth! Once, standing on our back piazza, I overheard my young cousin, then about eleven—my family, including my grandmother and two aunts, occupied three of the six flats at 31—improvising an ode to one of the blossoming pear trees: "Oh, you elegant tree!" she began. But then she caught my eye and the rhapsody was aborted. The contemplative and withdrawn could sit on the back piazzas and look at the fruit trees; the urban and the worldly could sit on the front piazzas and survey the passing scene.

I remember Providence Street best in the clear twilight of evenings in early summer. We boys had probably been for a swim at Jerry Daly's bath-house on Lake Quinsigamond. The long trudge back from the lake along Shrewsbury Street was easier than the walk to the lake; most of the four miles was downhill, for one thing. At the bottom of

Shrewsbury was the old Union Station, with its gray stone campanile tower. Past the grade crossing on Grafton Street we were practically home; the short length of Grafton Street led into Grafton Square at the base of Providence Street hill. On Grafton Square was Elkind's drug store; we would have a look in there on the chance that someone—an uncle or an older brother—would treat us to a soda.

Elkind's was smartly fitted up. It had tables with glass cases for tops; these cases contained boxes of Page and Shaw's chocolates to tempt us with solid sweets while we were imbibing liquid ones. During my childhood, Elkind's was the place we made for when we could beg, borrow or steal a nickel. What the country stores were in the early part of the nineteenth century, the drug stores became at the end of it in towns the size of Worcester; what the pubs are in English villages, Elkind's was for us. (Hard drinking was practically unknown on Providence Street; we boasted one drunk, and he was treated with a tolerant pity.) Elkind's was the forum for political, financial and social gossip; it was tavern, debating society, and even exchange. My uncles, who styled themselves "woolen merchants"—they were actually jobbers—went to the mills in such distant, fabulous places as Woonsocket and Providence and bought up remnants, odd lots, and damaged goods, and sold them in their shops on Winter Street. The manufacturers from New York would come up to buy from them and they sometimes sealed their bargains with a bumper at Elkind's.

Very near the bottom of the hill, on the right, was Cassie McMahon's house. She was an adorable young girl; her loveliness took your breath away. But she lived in a private house, a house all to herself and her parents, and this made her automatically unapproachable. She was sweet; she nodded and smiled at us, and then went back into her private house. She had no neighbors—that is to say, no other families living in her house to whom we could get close in order to get close to Cassie. She was isolated, which she didn't seem to mind; but we were isolated too, and this was grievous. For many decades I have promised myself that I would go back to find Cassie, but I have never done so. It is still on my unwritten psychic agenda.

Opposite Cassie's, on the left side, was the Providence Street school—our winter prison. And a little above that was the fire house. In summer we passed it with dim, luxurious memories of blizzardy winter mornings when we would lie in bed waiting for the "no-school" bells from the fire house. That sound induced a joy that no symphonic masterpiece of later years could possibly rival. But now it was early summer; long days of leisure stretched ahead of us into infinity and we were independent of school, independent of the fire house.

On the right, a little above Cassie's, was the first of Providence Street's two synagogues. This was a shabby wooden building. It was called the Balbirishocker Schul; its congregation was composed of emigrants from a town called, I suppose, Balbirishock. None of us—my father's set—ever went into it; our synagogue was august and made of brick with white limestone facings and was altogether more imposing than the humble little Balbirishocker Schul. Why Providence Street needed two synagogues I never knew. Not long ago I heard a story which, for the first time, made me understand why. It concerned a deeply religious man who was wrecked on an island off Tierra del Fuego. For eighteen years he lived alone on this island. Every morning he went to the shore and waved a white cloth in the hope of rescue. One morning he actually did signal a ship. The captain came ashore and the castaway showed him around the island. At one end was a quite substantial wooden building with a turret. "That," said the proud islander, "is the synagogue. I built it with my own hands!" They continued their tour. At the other end of the island, some miles away, the sightseeing captain saw another building, a replica of the first. "I built that too," said the castaway. "What on earth is it?" asked the captain. "That," said the pious craftsman loftily, "is the synagogue I *don't* go to!" We— the congregation of the Providence Street Synagogue—had the distinction of *not* going to the Balbirishocker Schul; the congregation of the latter could pride themselves on not going to ours. I suppose it gave each of the two factions a feeling of exclusiveness and privacy in their approach to God. Variety in worship adds, I suppose, to the color of life and is harmless if kept this side of slaughter; on Providence Street it usually was.

In summer the Providence Street car was open; when it was crowded, as it generally was at about the time we would be walking home from the lake, we could hitch a ride on it easily. We jumped on the running board and held on to one of the varnished posts and leaned far out into the whipped-up breeze. When the conductor saw us, we would drop off nonchalantly at the next stop as if we had just remembered an important engagement. If he didn't see us, we stayed on, though we were already late for supper: past all the intersecting streets; past the Polish Catholic Church at Waverly; past Jefferson, where stood the concrete mansion of the Croesus of the hill, Mr. Wolfson—the house with the stained-glass window; up and up to the crest of the hill, where Lovers Lane began. There the car-line stopped and we got off. We got off in another world.

Providence Street was crested with castles. One of these was the twelve-acre estate of the Cromptons. It was surrounded by a gray stone wall. Just inside the wall was an unbroken line of tall hemlocks. Above the trees we could see the great central tower of the mansion. The Crompton house was one of the first Elizabethan houses to be built in this country. Its wall braked the teeming life of our street, which came to a dead halt there. After the death of George Crompton, his sisters lived in the house, but no one ever saw them. The place was still; no sound ever came from it. But walking back home, brushing the wall as we passed it, stopping at the gates to look through the grill at the tree-lined walk that led to the great, many-windowed house, we could populate it at will from the story books we had been reading in and out of school.

A little below the Cromptons', across the street, was a walled town—a vast enclosure with fascinating, improbable, chocolate-colored turrets. This was the Worcester Academy. Inside the Crompton wall was one castle; inside the Academy walls were many, and they all seemed to us equally fabulous. The Academy was a private school which attracted students from all over the United States —mythical young men who could pay for their secondary educations. What manner of young men were these? What cities and families did they come from? We saw them—those of them who were on the Academy football and baseball teams were our heroes—but they were not real; they did not inhabit an actual world; they were as remote as the invisible inhabitants of the Crompton mansion. We even knew by sight the President of the Academy, Dr. Daniel Webster Abercrombie, who was one of the leading classical scholars in the country. But as far as being real to us was concerned, he might as well have lived in the Parthenon. He did, in fact, although it was called Davis Hall.

There was one other great demesne at the top of the hill—St. Vincent's Hospital. St. Vincent's was not walled. The great central red-brick building was set in a park. We saw the nuns scurrying about in this park and they were very friendly. My mother was always being hospitalized in St. Vincent's and she died there. She never could say enough in praise of the nuns. Though my mother spoke very little English, she managed to become firm friends with many of them. Whenever she came, they welcomed her. It was a charming consideration on the part of the nuns that they veiled the holy pictures on the walls—the Virgins and the Crucifixions—to spare the religious sensibilities of their orthodox Jewish patients.

My memory of all these summer twilights merges into a haze of warm felicity. But one of them I remember singly and vividly, since, as a gloomy German philosopher has said, we remember most clearly those things that have hurt us. On this particular evening I had been for a swim in Lake Quinsigamond, had dallied in Elkind's and had stolen a ride on the Providence Street car, intending to drop off in front of my house. But the conductor was absent-minded and I hung on till we got to the top of the hill. Lovers Lane looked especially inviting and I walked along for a bit under the great elms that met overhead. The silence was murmurous; the diamond light reflected from the leaves of the arching elms in green facets. I thought about my mother waiting for me with supper, turned back and started down the hill. I knew how she worried whenever I went to the lake. For a moment I hurried, but then I slowed down again. The immediate images, the teeming plans for the evening, were too compelling. I might go back to the lake for another swim—it had been brought up as a possibility that very afternoon. Someone might take me canoeing. Perhaps Morton Leavitt would be working in his father's shoe store, in which case Ada Summit, the siren of the hill, might be free. She might walk up Lovers Lane with me. The possibilities were dazzling. There was the night itself—a mystery that came from nowhere and under cover of which life took on a new coloration, a new shape, a new promise. Swimming in the lake at night was in a heightened category of experience, compared to swimming in it in the day time.

Next week would be the Fourth of July. The Maccabees Club next door to our house would be giving its annual party. Perhaps Ada Summit would come with me. A daring scheme formed in my mind: "Ask Ada Summit!" I was passing South Street. My Aunt Ida was sitting on her front piazza. She waved and called to me: "Spooning in Lovers Lane?" I nodded; it wouldn't do to tell Aunt Ida that I had been solitary. The abiding passion of her life centered in romance and its crystallization in marriage. Her piazza on South Street gave her a special vantage point; she could watch the young couples walking hand in hand, making their way toward the paradise of Lovers Lane. From her piazza she took the amorous pulse of the hill, and spotted prospects for her passionate avocation of matchmaking.

It was getting darker. The girls, more dutiful than I, had already had their suppers and were at the posts. The Providence Street mothers looked at the world from their balconies; their daughters surveyed it from the white-painted posts in the front yards. The more opulent of the triple-deckers (ours was not one) had little yards in front of them right up to the sidewalk. In the center of these yards were white-painted posts. Originally, probably, they were hitching posts; horses were not unfamiliar neighbors then. Against these posts the girls would lean, waiting for their steadies, or merely waiting. Several girls greeted me. They inquired whether I had had my supper. I had to say no; I remembered my waiting mother and hurried on. What were they doing later? They weren't sure. It was hazarded that we might see each other.

Then I saw Ada Summit. She was at her post. She gave me a ravishing smile. I stood before her, my heart beating.

"I was just thinking, Ada," I heard myself saying. I couldn't go on with it; I felt it was the wrong moment.

"What?" said Ada invitingly. "What were you thinking?"

"I was wondering . . ."

"What?"

"Who you're going to the Maccabees dance with . . ."

"That," said Ada provocatively, "is for me to know and for you to find out!"

I felt a fool and had a quick, throbbing sense of failure. I went on down the hill. My mother was standing in front of our house, tense with anxiety. So was I—about Ada.

Although, for some reason of pride, she always denied it, we all of us knew that Ada did have a steady. He was Morton Leavitt. Morton had the inside track. Morton was better off than the rest of us; Morton had spending money. He was a dandy and a card. He went away for vacations. He had been to Old Orchard Beach in Maine. He received travel folders. He had heard of Bermuda and talked airily of going there. He was good-looking and a snappy dresser—the Beau Brummel of the hill. Because, I suppose, of some excessive functioning of the salivary glands, there was always a slight foam at the corners of Morton's lips. The rest of us, who were very jealous of him, applied to him the sobriquet of "Spit" Leavitt. Even this he took as a kind of accolade. "Spit Leavitt made it," he would say of himself in terse summary of an anecdote of conquest.

Morton's hold over Ada Summit was complete. It amused Morton to demonstrate his power over Ada by allowing the rest of us, her unsuccessful lovers, to take her out occasionally when he had to work evenings at his father's shoe store on Harding Street—"The Shoe Mart"—during a holiday rush; or when he had what he would refer to mysteriously as "another engagement." He once gave me a nickel to take Ada to the Nickelodeon on Park Street, where the first silent pictures were playing. Afterwards, I had to deliver her back to Morton at the shoe store. Sometimes he would allow one of us to hold Ada's hand. He would take out a gold watch with an elaborately interwoven monogram of his initials on the case, and say: "Like to hold Ada's hand? Give him your hand, Ada, and let him hold it for a minute." Demurely, a little embarrassed, but smiling, Ada would offer her hand. Morton would stand, like a timekeeper, while you held Ada's hand. It was a kind of dispensed *droit du seigneur*, a demonstration to the world, as far as Ada was concerned, of Morton's power of total recall.

There was a devotional cult, among us small fry on Providence Street, for what we called "out-of-town" girls. An out-of-town girl automatically had overwhelming glamour simply because she didn't live in Worcester.

One June day there came into our midst a very unusual and heralded out-of-town girl, Miss Sawyer of Toronto. This was in itself noteworthy because Toronto was in Canada, which made Miss Sawyer the first foreign visitor to Providence Street. Moreover, she was a banker's daughter. With us the word "banker" was a synonym for a man of wealth beyond computing. Miss Sawyer and her father were to be house guests of the Wolfsons; Miss Sawyer's father was coming to look over Mr. Wolfson's comb factory with a view to refinancing and expanding it. The particular Fourth of July party after the arrival of Miss Sawyer of Toronto was memorable, packed with sensation.

The Maccabees was a social organization which actually had its own clubhouse next door to where we lived. It was a club organized by the older businessmen on the hill: my brother, Willie Lavin, and the rest were junior members. I hadn't the faintest idea what Maccabees were; it was not till many years later that I had reason to suspect that the founders of the club next door were not the original Maccabees. The earlier Maccabees, I was to discover, were a doughty crew who excelled in feats of arms. The Worcester ones were non-belligerent. They had officers whose terms lasted a year. The newly elected officials were inducted on the Fourth of July. They made speeches. After the oratory, there was ice cream and soft drinks and dancing in the light of the Japanese lanterns that were strung among the pear and apple and cherry trees. The trees were in full leaf and beneath them, under the Japanese lanterns, were long wooden trestles set out with refreshments. Inside the clubhouse a pianist and a banjoist were playing "On a Sunday Afternoon," "Moonlight Bay," "Take Me Out to the Ball Game" and other popular songs of the time. My crowd, the small fry, tried to infiltrate these parties and act like Maccabees.

On this particular Fourth of July, the lovely Myra Ellender, with whom the older set was in love as my set was in love with Ada Summit, came up and greeted me. She made me promise her a dance, which was generous of her, as I was a very uncertain dancer. I saw several girls and chatted with them, but I was miserable because they were not Ada. Ada, I was sure, would, of course, soon appear with Morton Leavitt. And suddenly I saw Ada; she was sitting wanly under a tree. She was, amazingly, alone. I went up to her and asked where Morton was. She shook her head miserably, but said nothing.

The music struck up, and I asked Ada to dance. She nodded listlessly, still without saying anything, and I walked with her into the clubhouse. The floor was densely crowded, which was a relief to me, because I was limited in maneuver. I wedged Ada into the swirl. After a few minutes, she asked me abruptly if I'd mind if we sat it out. As I led her off the floor to the rows of chairs ringed around the wall, I saw what she had just seen. Morton, grinning confidently, was leading Miss Sawyer onto the dance floor.

Willie Lavin, who, for some reason, had always taken a deep interest in me, sidled up to us. I had confided to Willie my passion for Ada. It had always irked Willie that I, whom he considered worthy to enter into deep discussions of large questions with him, whom he had encouraged to be a pianist, a debater, a philosopher, a puzzle-contest winner, and even a writer, should take second place with Ada Summit to a character like Morton Leavitt, whom he looked down upon as a Philistine and a shoe salesman, with what he contemptuously referred to as "superficial values." Strolling with me under the Japanese lanterns, he now gave me a heart-to-heart talk. The incident with Miss Sawyer, he said, was a godsend. It must reveal to Ada what a materialist, opportunist, will-o'-the-wisp Morton Leavitt was. Miss Sawyer, he understood, would be resident among us for two weeks. These two weeks presented me with a golden opportunity. It was the moment to rush in for the kill. By devoting myself to Ada for a fortnight, by allowing her to look deep into the cool depths of my character, I would make her, he ventured to say, wonder what she could ever have seen in a shallow fellow like Leavitt. "Why," he said, cracking his knuckles, a little idiosyncrasy of his, "I can well imagine a situation where Ada will thank her lucky stars that this incident hap-

51

pened, where she will look on Miss Sawyer's arrival as an act of Providence."

Suddenly, Willie took me by the arm and swerved me toward one of the windows of the clubhouse. He pointed to Miss Sawyer; she was abnormally tall; her somewhat pelican-like head bobbed over the other dancers. "Look at her!" he commanded. "Imagine giving up a beautiful girl like Ada for *that*! I will go so far as to say that Toronto or no Toronto, banker's daughter or no banker's daughter, Miss Sawyer is as homely as a hedge fence!" I gasped at such a heresy about an out-of-town girl and, moreover, a banker's daughter. When I looked at Miss Sawyer again, through Willie's eyes, I saw that there was something in what he said. That did it. I went back inside and sat by Ada, emboldened.

There followed a delirious two weeks when I occupied the proud and throbbing status of being Ada's steady. She was sweet. She was willing to see me every night, to go everywhere with me: canoeing; dancing in White City, the pleasure-dome on the lake; walking with me in Lovers Lane, or just sitting with me on her porch, on the warm summer evenings, watching the passing scene on the hill. Of course all this was very expensive. Taking Ada to the lake meant the additional cost of streetcar fare. When I went with my crowd, we always walked, but you couldn't expect Ada to walk. Then, canoes were expensive. Willie financed me.

One Saturday during these two weeks, I got the idea that I must take Ada to Rebboli's. Rebboli's was a fine confectioner's on Main Street. The moment I arrived with Ada I was aware of Miss Sawyer, looming up toward the crystal chandelier that hung from the center of the atelier. Morton sat possessively beside her. As we passed their table, Morton half rose; but Ada moved straight on. She cut him dead. Somewhat in a dither, conscious of moving uncertainly through a thick ambush of amorous intrigue, I piloted Ada to a table at the back. Somehow, the presence there of Morton and Miss Sawyer put a blight on this costly rendezvous. Somehow, although Ada had indeed been mine for two weeks, the relationship was never secure. Things hadn't gone quite as Willie predicted. Ada was adorable and kind, but she was abstracted. I felt increasingly that I was living on borrowed time.

I heard myself saying to Ada: "I suppose, after Miss Sawyer goes back to Toronto, you'll take up with Morton again."

"You needn't worry about that," Ada said tensely. "I never want to see Morton again. I hate him!"

That afternoon, when I took her home, Ada unaccountably pleaded with me to save the following Tuesday night for her. I promised, of course, but I was bewildered by her request because I was seeing her every night anyway. The next day, though, the gossips of our crowd shed some light on it. Miss Sawyer was returning to Toronto on Tuesday. I thought then that I saw the reason for Ada's insistence about seeing me Tuesday, and the conclusion I reached was not cheering. Ada had known that Miss Sawyer was leaving; she had divined that on that night Morton would be free and might ask to see her. She had not been able to rely on her own strength or pride to refuse, and she wished to have an engagement with me in order to be able to say that she was busy. My heart sank. The intensive and costly courtship was a failure; Willie, the *éminence grise* of the maneuver, had underestimated Morton's power; to Ada, evidently, Morton's values were anything but superficial!

My dates with Ada between then and Tuesday were agonizing; there was no joy in them for either of us. On Tuesday night, however, I went to her house at the appointed time. I walked into the living room and there was Morton. He was sitting on the sofa with Ada. Ada looked happy for the first time since the arrival of Miss Sawyer. As for Morton, he was in wonderful fettle; he jumped to his feet and beamed at me like a welcoming committee. He took out his gold watch to note the time. "Like to hold Ada's hand?" he said. "Forty-five seconds?"

With each spring, our thoughts turned to baseball and girls. Beneath the oppressive religiosity at home, these were tidal preoccupations, loosening the cinctures of the Providence Street school. The members of the Worcester Academy baseball team were our childhood heroes; the arc had not yet widened to include the team of Holy Cross, which was strong enough to combat Yale and Harvard and the Carlisle Indians. We watched for the appearance of the Academy players on the Providence Street car, hung around the walled city of the Academy to catch a glimpse of them, and, before their games, we were in a state of feverish excitement.

But we had baseball teams of our own and an arena of our own. This was a barren, uneven, and gravelly abandoned lot, gleaming here and there with bits of sharp quartz—I think it may have been an abandoned quarry—that was called, with a singular excess of poetic license, Swan's Field. We made for the field directly after school was over; we played through the long twilights till our eyes strained to see the ball; our mothers could not get us home for supper. There would be accidents: a sprained ankle and a torn ligament—and our mothers came to look on Swan's Field as an enemy, a zone of peril, which they feared as they did Lake Quinsigamond and the hazards of canoeing. But nothing could keep us away from Swan's Field.

Correspondence with the sporting goods houses was an absorbing corollary; we discussed endlessly the grain of bats, the stitching and fillings of balls, the toughness and resilience of catchers' mitts, the cleats on shoes. (Morton Leavitt was able to send for cleated shoes.) Spaulding and Ditson vied for our

custom. We pored over the illustrations in their catalogues, arguing endlessly the relative merits of
their products, though there was very little chance
of our acquiring any of these cherished objects. We
were like art-lovers too impecunious to buy masterpieces.

In our set, in those days, there was only one
index of status: prowess on Swan's Field. Before
each game, the captains of our scrub teams assigned
the places. I have said that Swan's Field was
uneven. This is imprecise as well as merciful to that
old lot on which so many of our hopes and ambitions were centered. It was not uneven; it was cor-
rugated, lop-sided, craggy. There was a fair plateau
in the center—the pitcher's mound—and beyond
that a great terrain that looked like the craters of the
moon. Here the infield functioned. Beyond that,
though, Swan's Field gave up. It ran away, at first
tentatively, in a gradual descent, and then abruptly,
down a canyon. Because we found out early that to
recover balls that were hit over this canyon took up
too much valuable time, we evolved a convention
that a ball that wasn't stopped before it went over
must be considered a foul. The first decline, the
gradual one, was so far away from center in any
case, that it was almost academic what happened
out there. We didn't assign right and left and center;
we dubbed the region loosely "The Outfield" and
assigned one stalwart to cover it. The post was a
sinecure. Whoever was assigned to it could see very

little of what was going on in the diamond. He had to stand pretty far up the slope to see the heads of the pitcher or the batter.

In baseball I won my place early. I was near-sighted and inept. I practiced throwing by the hour in our backyard, in a mounting fury at my own inadequacy. I simply could not learn to throw with accuracy. And yet I fed myself constantly with the illusion that there was a secret, a trick, which, once I mastered it, would make a thrower of me. I never learned this secret (I wasn't a very good batter either) and yet I was in the game because there was no place in our society for anyone who was not in the game. I was up on the catalogues with the best of them; I knew where Spaulding was strong and Ditson weak and vice-versa. I knew intimately the personnel of the Worcester Academy teams and what might be expected of them in their next Saturday's contests with Exeter or Andover. I was an informed connoisseur. But it didn't help my throwing arm. I trotted along with the others to Swan's Field. The captains changed and the positions varied at the whim of each captain. But whoever was captain, I soon became aware, indulged in no vagaries about me. I was automatically assigned the Outfield. I came to expect it and I came to dread it. A lot depended, for my writhing amour propre, on the intonation with which the dread assignment was enunciated. A sweet fellow, like Dave Seder, made a feint of thinking it over. He would purse his lips and ponder and finally say: "Sam—The Outfield," as if he had given the matter close thought and only relegated me to this banishment after having weighed me carefully in his mind for more important posts. Captain Morton Leavitt, on the other hand, had no such consideration for my sensibilities. He would wave me at once to the outfield with a knowing smirk. It was my bad luck to have Morton as my captain a few days after the incident with the stopwatch. I remember that day. It was a long walk to the outfield. Once there, it was lonely.

On Saturdays and holidays there was exaltation in going "down the line"—the expression we used for going downtown. Past Elkind's, down Grafton, down Front, past the Common with its statue of the great Massachusetts Senator, George Frisbie Hoar; past the City Hall, to Easton's, at Main and Pleasant. The trek from the soda fountain at Elkind's to the soda fountain at Easton's was a long leap in evolution because Easton's was the center of the world. (Londoners, I somewhat incredulously discovered later, cherished the fond illusion that it was Piccadilly Circus; they just didn't know Easton's!) The displacement of the pass-word for rendezvous from "meet you at Elkind's" to "meet you at Easton's" signalized the transition from the periphery to the core, from provincialism to worldliness, from naiveté to sophistication. I remember Colonel Easton; he was one of the most imposing men I have ever seen: tall and courtly, with a white goatee. My Aunt Ida once wrote rhapsodically to a young woman in Norfolk, Virginia, describing an offered bridegroom: "I tell you he's beautiful—like Colonel Easton—with a little dyke beard, only black not white!" It was beyond my aunt's generous imagination to conceive a heroine so benighted that she would not instantly acknowledge Colonel Easton—whom she had never seen—as the fixed gauge of manly beauty.

A few streets down from Easton's was Pleasant, where the Worcester Public Library was—an outlet to the universe. On Main Street was the gloomy cavern of Mechanics Hall, where Presidents spoke and great artists performed. A few blocks below that was Exchange and the Worcester Theatre, where you could behold the avatars of glamour by paying twenty-five cents for a seat in the second balcony.

Our street, Providence, led to all these streets. And these led to country roads and these country roads led to other streets. And these streets were in other cities which lay beyond one's reach, but capturable through some not impossible twist in the veiled future. Palmer and Springfield, Ware and Woonsocket, Northampton and Framingham— what manner of places were these? There were no motor cars then and the roads that led to these far cities could not be burned up; they had to be travelled, they had to be traversed. We knew we would come to them in time, these strange places; they would be conquered in time; they beckoned from the haze and shimmer of the horizon.

The evocation of these names haunts me still. When I see them from train windows even now, I am brought up short: "Can this really be Palmer? Am I really in Palmer?" They are still the far points of the world. There is only one street, indivisible as the sea, which touches every shore. The horizon widens, the horizon contracts. It remains the same.

3

MALACH HAMOVES

Our tenement on Providence Street, besides housing my parents, my two older brothers, and me, was heavily populated with angels. Every night, as I was falling asleep in the bedroom I shared with one of my brothers, I would hear my father, through the door that separated me from the kitchen, pacing back and forth and intoning in Hebrew his evening prayer, which he would repeat three times. Its mournful cadences ended with the words by which, before committing himself to sleep, he invoked attendant presences: ". . . and may the Angel Michael be at my right hand; Gabriel on my left; before me, Uriel; behind me, Raphael; and over my head the divine presence of

61

God."

As long ago as I can remember, I was acutely aware of this quartet of angels and felt that their general disposition was protective and friendly; indeed, I often called upon them to help me in my desperate nocturnal wrestlings with a fifth, and sinister, angel, who also, and unwelcomely, persisted in staying with us on Providence Street. This was the Malach Hamoves, the Angel of Death, a familiar character in Jewish folklore, who was very real to me because of the constant references to him in the conversation of my father and his friends. The very sound of his name was dark, hooded, penetrating, and the personality it evoked gelid and implacable. Somehow, against him, Michael and Gabriel, Uriel and Raphael seemed to be, with all the good will in the world, of small avail. Though often, in my nightly struggles with their opposite number, they entered my room en masse to assist me, their joined strengths invariably proved unequal to the agonizing climactic tussle. Even when my own screams woke me while the battle was at its tensest and the outcome not yet decided, I always had a horrid feeling that if the struggle had continued even a moment longer, the issue, in spite of the good offices of my four friends, would have been decided in favor of the Evil One.

How lightly the four good angels were regarded in Providence Street is illustrated by an anecdote about them that I heard first when I was so young I could only dimly apprehend it. It concerned an excessively pious lady who had married a gentleman less devout. It was the bride's habit to repeat the evening prayer three times before she went to bed. The worldling, lounging in bed one night, found the long procession of holy presences oppressive and protested with some petulance, "You invite in so many angels, there'll be no room in bed for me!" As I grew older, I, too, came to feel for the quartet a kind of affectionate contempt—at least when I thought of them in the daytime. But when they made their entrance into my father's prayer as I was dozing off at night, they were somewhat more formidable. Their presence brought sharply to mind, with a tightening of fear, the hovering figure of their malevolent colleague. Were they, these four, really so amiable? Why, then, did they follow the same profession as the Malach Hamoves, who by his intractability and venom gave the whole company a dubious name? Still, my father had such confidence in the four and implored them with such fervor to attend him that I, though with less confidence, joined in the petition. In so hard a pass as mine during my struggle with the Other, I was glad of help from any quarter, and I consoled myself with the thought that the four would in good time come to my aid. But here, too, I felt a sinking of the heart. They were *too* amiable. Their very good will, I felt, rendered them impotent in the impending struggle. This was the genesis, perhaps, of a cynical idea I had to combat later—that the good cannot also be powerful.

The form of my struggle—its terrain and its tactics—was always the same. It was a fixed dream of horror, which came to me early in the evening, before my older brother had come into our room to go to bed. It had settled upon me when I first began to have a dim notion of what death meant. Perhaps my antagonist was the more vividly embodied for me because my mother, from the earliest time I can remember, was intermittently pronounced to be dying. She suffered from asthma, and her prolonged suffocations in her incense-laden room were struggles I identified as daytime versions of my own nocturnal bouts with the Malach Hamoves. When I was allowed to see her during an attack, she would be either sitting up in her bed struggling for breath or walking about trying, as I understood from my own experience, to shuffle off her tormentor, and I wondered why she scattered her energies thus instead of focussing her strength, as I did at night, on remaining flat on the bed, inviolate.

Sometimes, on late-summer or early-fall nights, after a day of swimming or canoeing at Lake Quinsigamond, I would go to bed exhausted and drowse, pleasantly at first, revolving in my mind the hazards and excitements of the day, and anticipating already that moment in the morning when the other boys would pick me up for the long trudge to the lake. And then there would come through to me from the next room my father's measured pacing and the creak of the floor boards while he intoned, softly but distinctly, his prayer. The words, although I did not understand them all, had become familiar to me, syllable by syllable, and their cadence was so unvarying that it took the place of words that had meaning. Their unbroken modulation was always sad, but it was also soothing. This sedative effect lasted until, at the very end of the prayer, the four made their entrance. By this time, I had moved too far toward sleep to turn back, but I held on desperately to the filaments of consciousness until the four should reappear, when my father repeated the prayer. I knew that to lose hold entirely left me open to the stern visitation from the Other, and I fought off sleep because I did not want to be alone when he came. Before long, I would hear the familiar names again, though more dimly, following my father in drowsy processional as he circled the kitchen—Michael and Gabriel, Uriel and Raphael. These four names, at least, were friendly and reassuring. But what was the proper name of their co-worker and what, in off hours, did his friends call him? It struck me bleakly that he had no familiar name, he had no off hours. His black title was his specialty. Nightly I vowed that *this* time I would be prepared for his appearance in advance, *this* time I would actually see the nameless one cross the threshold of my room and be ready to spar with him. Yet I was never able to achieve that active vigilance. Never once, in my numberless encounters, did I see the Malach Hamoves make his entrance. He always just materialized and was standing by my bed, looking down at me.

He was monkish, soberly gowned, and very tall, with a long, thin face and an expression that was detached and not in the least hostile. This impersonality was the most terrifying thing about him. One knew at once that he was beyond argument and that, ultimately, he would have to be met by force. He would stand motionless by my bed for a long time, looking down at me. My first maneuver was to roll to the other side of the bed, as far away from him as I could get, but I would find him standing at that side then, gazing down at me. At first, he did not reach out his hands to take me or even beckon to me, but because I knew what was about to happen, I dug in for the siege. My tactics were purely defensive—quite literally a holding action. I slept on a white-painted iron bed. The headboard was a frame with short posts at each side that terminated in the unexpected elegance of brass knobs. The metal runners that supported the bedspring were round and easy to grasp. Since it was the Angel's object to get me out of bed and take me away with him, I would turn on my side and seize a runner with one hand and with the other clutch the brass knob over my head. This position, a sort of lopsided crucifixion, was awkward and eventually fatiguing, but it meant that I was already holding on ferociously when the Angel reached out to take me. There followed a tug of war. Oddly enough, I could not feel the Angel's hands; although they gripped mine to pry them loose, there was no contact of flesh. The force he exerted was not a matter of physical contact but a kind of suction, in which I felt myself gradually being drawn off. I held on for dear life, until the pain in my fingers and knuckles became almost insupportable. To hold on to some part of the bed, to maintain contact with it, became the essence of survival, and the bed seemed to be the only familiar thing in a swirling and fearsome unknown. Sometimes, when the contest approached its climax, the four friendly angels would come in and try to neutralize the determination of my antagonist, but they were ineffectual and he ignored them, concentrating on me. They fell upon him and melted like snowflakes. In fact, I proved hardier than they. Yet a moment always came when I knew I had to give in and felt my fingers begin to relax. I was lost, and awoke screaming.

I remember wondering, when I was told that someone had died, whether he had not resisted the Angel of Death, as I had, and whether he might have lived if he had simply held on to his bed and refused to be dislodged. Before we moved to

Providence Street, we had lived on Water Street, and there, one afternoon, my sister, who was only a year older than I, had run out into the street to play and had been killed by a streetcar. Somehow, except for the reflection I got of it in my mother's grief, this event did not really affect me; it was an accident and therefore not an expression of my familiar angel's professional malevolence. My mother's prolonged dying was different; that did relate, and directly, to my own experience, for I saw that her suffering was also a contest, and I deplored, though I could never bring myself to tell her so, what seemed to me a lamentable feebleness in her technique of evasion.

One night during an unusually severe attack of my mother's, I was lying in bed and heard my father and my brothers, in the kitchen, repeating in hushed voices what our family physician, Dr. Jim Nightingale, had told them—that they must prepare for the worst, that my mother would probably not live through the night. I instantly determined to go in and tell her just what to do; I even imagined myself fixing her hand tightly on one of the rails and then closing my own hand over hers and sitting through the night with her, keeping her hands thus double-locked against the adversary. But while I was planning these heroics, I was overtaken by sleep and was soon engaged in my own tussle.

My father must have not gone to bed at all that

night, for I did not hear his prayer, but I did not need the entrance of the amiable four to evoke the Other, since he was in the flat already. As I dropped off, I even felt a kind of security, because I was sure the Black Angel must be busy in my mother's room. But in a few moments, when I saw him standing beside me, I realized, with a sinking of the heart, that his activities were multifarious; he had time for me, too! Then it occurred to me that perhaps my mother's case was easier now that I had drawn off her tormentor. Whatever comfort this gave me was soon blotted out in the stringency of my own battle. It went on for a long time, soundlessly and mercilessly, and, for the first time, the Angel seemed personally ferocious. There grew in me the sense that if he won over me, he would win over my mother, too, and my determination to hold on tightened indomitably. I knew that on other occasions I had screamed; this time I must not scream, for my mother would hear it and might take it as a signal to capitulate.

When I could hold on no longer and was about to cry out, I was awakened by my father. To my surprise, I could see the first morning light coming in the windows. My father stood where the Angel had stood. His face was gray. I waited for him to tell me that my mother was dead. I was afraid that even though I had won, she had lost. But my father said only that my mother was very bad; he wanted me to get dressed quickly and go with him to fetch

Dr. Nightingale while my brothers stayed with my mother.

Dr. Jim Nightingale was held in affectionate awe by the residents of Providence Street. To them, he was a figure of scandal and mystery. I was not old enough to take this in quite, at the time my mother was so sick, but as I grew up on Providence Street, I assimilated the doctor's story. He was ribald, but he was also erudite and endlessly devoted to his patients. He played the oboe, which struck them as a singular avocation for an overworked general practitioner, and went to Boston once a week to take lessons from the chief oboist of the Boston Symphony Orchestra. People shrugged their shoulders at this perversion. Wasn't it an accepted fact that Nightingale, though a wonderful doctor, was crazy? Jim, as my elders called him, and as I came to think of him, was a bachelor, which to Providence Street was eccentric, and he was invariably accompanied on his rounds by a cadaverous young man, whom he referred to as his assistant. This assistant was a tall, incredibly emaciated, goggle-eyed diabetic, who had come to the doctor as a patient when he was sixteen and remained to work for him until the young man died, twelve years later. I was at first terrified of this skeleton, but when I was given "The Legend of Sleepy Hollow" to read in the Providence Street School, I immediately identified him with Ichabod Crane. After that, I felt better about him. Among the hushed whispers concerning Dr. Nightingale was one to the effect that he used Ichabod for experimental purposes, in order to find a cure for diabetes. The truth, as I was to discover later, was more prosaic. The boy was an orphan and penniless, and if he hadn't become Jim Nightingale's assistant, it was difficult to imagine what he would have done; Jim gave him the job out of sheer kindness. Ichabod would sit in Jim's buggy, holding the reins, while the doctor was inside making his calls, and when Jim came out with his little black bag and climbed aboard, Ichabod would cluck up the horse and drive off. On summer evenings, anyone who strolled past Dr. Nightingale's office could hear the mournful mewings of his oboe and see his assistant sitting on the black leather sofa in the waiting room listening, expressionless. In all the years I saw the doctor's assistant, I never heard him say a word.

Everything about Dr. Nightingale—his personal appearance, his horse and buggy, and his office, which was also his home—was rather sloppy. He was quite short, his skin was very dark, and his ruddy cheeks were the color of black oxheart cherries. He laughed easily and had great, merry black eyes. He liked children and he gave the Providence Street kids the run of his office. We used to pore over his medical books; the illustrations in the obstetrical tomes were prime favorites. His office was also a kind of negligently managed private museum, in which the objects on display ran the gamut of the doctor's dissolving hobbies. The walls were covered with framed butterflies that he had collected and mounted himself. There were filing cabinets containing colored cards on which he had transcribed quaint prescriptions and medical references from sixteenth-century English literature. He was always planning to write a book to be called *Medical References in Elizabethan Literature*, and these cards were his notes for it, but he never got around to writing the book. Jim's waiting room was the only one in my experience that had a piano in it. The music rack of his upright was covered with Mozart and Beethoven sonatas. He played the piano, but he said he played it badly—his instrument was the oboe. The other major object in the waiting room was an extremely dilapidated black leather sofa, on which he slept at night. His friends were always asking the doctor whether he couldn't afford to buy a new sofa to replace this one, which sagged more and more over the years as his patients sat on it, and Jim would reply amiably that he would much rather get rid of his patients than of his sofa. Then he would go on to make tantalizing, enigmatic remarks about the sofa, attributing its odd curvatures to the exercise of his seductive prowess. Ichabod occupied a room, no larger than a closet, that opened off the office and was full of surgical instruments. People used to ask Jim whether he wasn't afraid of his assistant's cutting himself at night on one of these instruments. "If he does," he'd say airily, "he won't bleed."

The ladies of Providence Street, particularly, adored Dr. Nightingale; to them, he represented romance as well as mystery. He would tease them unmercifully and call them hypochondriacs. When they telephoned him to tell him about their colds and beg him to call, he would tell them that there was nothing wrong with them and that he needed the time for patients who were really sick. If he did call, he would as likely as not make light of their ailments. "The truth is you're bored with your husband and crave my society," he would say. Or he would get up abruptly and shut off an inventory of trivial symptoms with the taunt "How long do you expect me to stay and listen to you for a dollar?" or "Why don't you go to a fancy, two-dollar doctor? He'll listen to you forever."

I left the house with my father to fetch Dr. Nightingale at a little before five that morning. It was early September; the leaves of the trees were still a summer green, and there lingered among the branches a faint, milky fog, which the sun had not yet washed away, although the floating wisps were already translucent with pink light. My father said nothing as we walked down the steep, silent Providence Street hill. I saw his lips move; he was muttering something to himself. The air was soft and full, but with an intimation of sharpness, an edge of something that was not summer. I was conscious of the prodigality of the air, so abundant and ample and circumambient; perhaps this consciousness was heightened by the realization that my mother was in her room suffocating for lack of it. The outlines of the buildings we passed were sharp against the sky: the Catholic church, with its cross; the somewhat grandiose, curved twin staircases that led to the puny façade of our synagogue; the commonplace flat rooftop of the Providence Street School. In the limpid melting-together of summer and fall, there was the fullness of expectancy and the merest hint of farewell. The fear of death had never been so vivid to me before, nor has it ever been since, and yet I felt, as I walked down the hill, a kind of pride in my own indestructibility and a certain impatience with my mother for dying. I was proud because in my recent contest I had won out without screaming; I had in me a tenacity that my mother evidently lacked. And, too, the doctor had said that she might die—and people did die. I knew what it was to struggle with death; I did not know, nor could I imagine, what it was to die. What it was like if you lost out was a fearsome speculation.

The brass plaque bearing the legend "James Nightingale, M.D." was filmed with dew when we pressed the electric button beneath it. The doctor opened the door almost at once; he already had his trousers on and was slipping his suspenders over his shoulders. He must have grabbed the trousers the moment he heard our steps on the little stoop. Through the open office door, I saw Ichabod emerging from his closet. Nobody said anything; it was a dream scene in dumb show. Ichabod went to the barn, and we waited until he brought the horse and buggy to the curb. Jim and my father squeezed in beside him, Ichabod clucked, and the equipage creaked off. I returned on foot. On the way back, I wondered whether my mother would be dead when I arrived and, if so, what she would look like. My own sense of immortality intensified. I breathed deep of the now warmer and still more gracious air, as if to demonstrate my capacity for unlimited inhalation. Suddenly, the whole idea of my mother's problem became infinitely remote, even uninteresting. Definitely, death was the concern of other people.

But when I reached our tenement, this cavalier attitude vanished, for the Dark Angel, the Tireless One, was inside, and he had a victim who was without my experience or technical skill. I had no faith whatever in Jim Nightingale. I had seen him carry that little black satchel of his into our house so often that what it contained seemed to me to have no potency. You could not put the Angel off with pills or instruments or stratagems. It was a question of will, a question of strength. Ichabod sat in the buggy, his vacant eyes staring at nothing. He appeared to have no vitality whatever and I felt that the Angel could dispose of him with a flick of his wrist; if he hadn't done so already, it was merely because it hadn't been worth his while. I had a deep wish not to go into the house, for I was sure everything was over and I was afraid of seeing, for the first time, the Angel's handiwork. But I felt an obligation. If my mother was still alive, I had to help her. I had to infuse her with my own indestructibility and convey to her what I had learned from practical experience.

She was sitting up in her bed, propped against a stack of pillows. The air of the room was damp and heavy with foreign matter. On earlier occasions when my mother was sick and I had wanted to go in to see her, I had often been shooed out. This time nobody said a word. My father and my brothers stood around the bed, watching. My first thought was: Why don't they take her outside, where the air is so abundant and accessible? Since no one stopped me, I moved closer to the bed. Dr. Nightingale was sitting beside it, holding my mother's wrist. Her eyes were closed and her face was tilted up, as if she were trying to reach some untapped reservoir of air. As I came to the side of the bed, she opened her eyes and looked at me. I hoped for recognition, for a ghost of her unfailing smile, but she closed her eyes again as though she had not seen me. This frightened me and, for a moment, I felt helpless. Dr. Nightingale let her wrist fall, turned to the others, and shook his head, as if he felt helpless too. It seemed to me that this was my opportunity. I would close her hand over the iron rail of the frame and clasp it there, held in my own. I would never let go. But when I looked at her hand I was shocked, because I saw that it was limp and enervated. I could not relate it to my mother's hand as I knew it, deft and nimble at the stove or at her sewing. It was not her hand, or anyone's hand, and I was suddenly aware that it already belonged to the Antagonist and could not join in an alliance against him. I looked at my mother's face. It was still her face. In a dreadful apprehension that any moment I might see it become as helpless as her hand, I ran out of the room and out of the house into the airy, delicious early morning.

Impertinently flouting Dr. Nightingale's prediction, my mother survived that night. Then there gradually grew in the family circle a conviction that there was only one way in the world to lift her out of the twilight between life and death in which she hovered. This was to send her to New York, to see Professor Abraham Jacobi. I don't know exactly how it had come about, but Providence Street throbbed with talk of the renown of Professor Jacobi. I have since learned that Professor Jacobi was indeed a very considerable man, but I have never been able to determine just how Providence Street came to have so exalted an opinion of his ability. He was primarily a pediatrician, and why my family should have made the great sacrifice it took to send an adult asthmatic to see him is still mysterious. It may have been simply that on Providence Street the name of Professor Jacobi was uttered with a reverence second only to that offered the Deity Himself. Jim Nightingale had the tremendous disadvantage, as a practitioner, of living in Worcester, while Professor Jacobi had never done anything more demeaning than to practice briefly and unsuccessfully in Boston. And he had lived that down by his enormous success in New York. It may be that his local renown was started by my Aunt Ida. It was Aunt Ida who, when she married my Uncle Harry and moved from Boston to Worcester, brought the first word of Professor Jacobi's fame. The Professor had been imprisoned in the German Revolution of 1848, had come to this country in the eighteen-fifties, and had, Aunt Ida claimed, once cured her father, in a trice, of something incurable. In any case, the pressure on the family to send my mother to see him in New York became irresistible. The reason for this was that, beyond anything my Aunt Ida or anyone else could have said about him, Professor Jacobi had in his favor one overwhelming and Olympian characteristic that, in itself, was enough to strike Providence Street mute with awe. This was the simple fact that he was a German.

It is difficult to convey the prestige enjoyed by Germans among the Russian-born citizens of Providence Street; it surpassed even the prestige in which they were held, in the middle of the last century, by Emerson and the Transcendentalists, thirty miles away from Worcester, in Concord. On Providence Street, it was said of Professor Jacobi, in a hushed voice, "*Er iz a Daitsch*," and that was enough. It was as much as to say, "He is a prophet, an encyclopedist; he is Galen, Aesculapius, Spinoza." Later in life, I actually got to know some Germans, and I was to discover that they could be stuffy as well as learned, but in my childhood I joined in the pervasive, unmitigated worship of everything German. To send my mother to New York entailed rigid family economy over a long period, nor was it easy to get an appointment with the Professor, who was, by this time, an extremely busy man. The appointment was made, finally, by Aunt Ida's father, the Ramaz, who was by then also practicing in New York, at the Congregation Kehilath Jeshurun, on East Eighty-fifth Street. My mother went off, escorted by my Uncle Harry, to keep it. She made several such trips. On her return from each of them, Providence Street's curiosity about Professor Jacobi far exceeded its interest in what he had done for her. What was it like to be examined by a German? What did Professor Jacobi look like? I remember my mother's saying that he was a short man. Suddenly, to be short seemed ultimately desirable. My Uncle Harry, who was tall, hung his head in shame.

Whether it was due to the curative effects of being permitted to pay a fee to a German, or to some obscure cellular process that no one knew anything about, or perhaps, even, to the humble ministrations of Jim Nightingale, my mother gradually outgrew her attacks and, although she continued to look frail, she became perfectly well. She outlived her three sisters, and all but one of her four brothers. She and I both eluded our tormentor; by the time she was well, I was in high school and my dreams had swerved from battles with the Angel of Death to terrestrial, local combats—to Swan's Field, where we played baseball, and to the football games played on the crest of Providence Street hill, where I prayed passionately for the valiants of Worcester Academy.

Among certain of us boys on Providence Street, the desire to sleep away from home was obsessive, and so was the curiosity about—and the desire to penetrate—the immense, ill-defined area known as "out of town." My indulgence of this curiosity caused my mother I know not what agonies. I had an adventurous crony named Allie Price, who was ingenious in devising ruses for getting out of sleeping at home. He had the startling idea, one summer day, that he and I should sleep that night in Bancroft Tower. We did it. Bancroft Tower was built, I suppose, in memory of George Bancroft, the historian, who was born in Worcester, or of his preacher father, Aaron. It is constructed solidly of New England granite, and it might have been built by the Vikings as far as sleeping arrangements are concerned. I told my mother I was going to spend the night at Allie's house, and Allie told his mother he was going to spend it at mine. My mother happened to meet Mrs. Price at the grocery, where they compared notes, and my mother sat up all night waiting for me to return. Allie and I found that whatever you might do in Bancroft Tower, you couldn't sleep in it. We did our best; we got through the night somehow. When I returned to Providence Street in the morning, my mother was standing in front of our tenement house, wan and suffering. She did not reproach me, but every other member of the family did.

Another night, the fertile Allie got the idea that it would be a thrill to sleep in the Providence Street synagogue, which was then being rebuilt. As the pews hadn't been put in, it was hardly more comfortable than the Tower; I still remember the insomniac flapping of the canvas that had been stretched over the as yet eyeless rose window. How I got the requisite sense of adventure from this night, I don't know, since the synagogue was directly across the street from our tenement. At any rate, on both these nights I was immune from angelic visits, because it was impossible to sleep at all.

Allie's climactic improvisation was that we should run away to New York by streetcar. I told my mother we were going to make a visit in Ware, where Allie had relatives. We did go to Ware, and from there on to New York. We had twenty dollars between us, which took us to New York, kept us there for four days, and brought us back. We stayed in the Mills Hotel, on Thirty-sixth Street, which overawed us with its elegance and luxury. It was certainly more comfortable than Bancroft Tower. Near the end of our stay, the long arm of coincidence stretched out to give Allie and me a frightful moment. It was during the presidential campaign of 1908. We heard a band and saw a crowd in Madison Square, and amiably joined it. Pushing to the front of the throng, we stood at the foot of a temporary platform, receptive to political argument. To our horror, we found ourselves being invited to vote for Taft by one of my brothers' closest friends, Jack Asher (later Judge Asher). It was incredible, but there he was. Jack was studying law at Columbia at that time, and that speech in Madison Square must have been the very beginning of what turned out to be a lifetime career of trying to elect Republicans. For a few moments, Allie and I were transfixed with fear. Then we fled, hoping he had not seen us. This incident took the joy out of our trip, and we started home early the next morning. My parents found out about this expedition, too, and my father's anger was so great that my mother suffered almost as much from it as from my escapade.

My father was an unworldly, scholarly, casuistical, and normally gentle man with a supernatural imagination that dwelt mainly on the hereafter. Among the elders of the synagogue, he was considered an authority on Hebrew and on religious literature. He also taught the children of the neighborhood the Hebrew scriptures; the kitchen of our tenement was his schoolroom. His own ritualistic observances and studies were so exhaustive that he had little time left for what to him were the external and intrusive demands of life. To me and my brothers, he was tender and threatening by turns, but threatening only because he was himself threatened by a Master who required endless obeisance. He was the personal deputy, in our house, of a minatory Deity. I was not exactly afraid of my father, but I did fear the Interests he represented. I was closer to my mother, and had an adoration for her that I never felt for my father. How much my mother really believed, in the religious sense, I never knew. She was little and quiet; it was said that for a long time after my sister was killed, she didn't speak a single word. She had blue eyes and soft brown hair. I remember being grateful that she did not, like the pious ladies of her generation, wear the disfiguring *shaitels*, or wigs, required by ritual. Ladies were supposed not to be too alluring, because it would detract from what should be their main preoccupation—God. Perhaps my mother was proud of her hair; I know that I was. From the beginning, I sensed, dimly, that the gulf separating me from my father separated her from him also, and that because of this we had a kind of suppressed, conspiratorial alliance. Our communion, like the course of lovers, was starred with happiness and pain. Bitternesses sprang up between us, during which she never said much, whereas I was always voluble about my grievances and would lather myself up in self-justification and self-pity. And because I was the youngest and did not have to go to work as early as my older brothers had had to, I was at home more and saw more of her than they did. I believe I was the only one in the family with whom she had a relationship that, in its sunniest moments, might be described as gay. I could make her laugh, and she came to expect me to.

I developed a routine, for instance, of following her about while she was engaged in her household tasks, tagging at her heels so closely that her work was impeded. She would go into the pantry and I would follow; she would wash a dish and her elbow would hit me. She would then try to shoo me away, muttering the Yiddish word *"Meshugeneh"* ("crazy one"), but I was not to be put off by epithets. These long pantomimes would end only when she broke into helpless laughter. A diffi-

culty between us that lasted to the end was the bar-
rier of language. My mother spoke no English.
When I was small, I spoke Yiddish at home, but by
the time I went to high school, I had a conscious
revulsion from the language of my parents. I felt
that to speak it was a social denigration and that
Yiddish was an ugly tongue. I detested its sound
and its rhythms as compared to the sound and the
rhythms of English. I knew, also, that it was a bas-
tard version of the pure, Elysian, coveted German.
As I began to study German in high school, I
became the more acutely aware of the vulgariza-
tion of it we spoke at home, and when I heard
Yiddish or spoke it myself, it was with a sense of
shame. Not until long afterward did I come to realize what an extraordinarily responsive medium it
is for pathos and warmth of feeling and, above all,
for earthy and untranslatable humor.

One morning, when I was a freshman at Clark
College, in Worcester, I left the house as usual after
breakfast to go to classes. My father was sitting at
the kitchen table poring over one of his Talmudic
books—those big volumes bound in purple-veined
imitation calf that were seldom out of his hand
when he was at home. He gravely repeated, as I left
him, his invariable valediction in Hebrew: "Go in
peace, come back in peace." At ten o'clock that
morning, after my first class, I had a study period.
It was a radiant October day. I left the main building and started across the campus toward the cor-

ner drug store for a milk shake. Halfway across, I was aware of a sudden, curious malaise. The sun was warm, I was feeling all right; I slowed down, wondering what was the matter. Then I stopped, and, without knowing why, I decided to go to the library to study. On the way to the library, the strange feeling became more intense; I tried, unsuccessfully, to analyze it. When I got to the library, an attendant told me that there was a message for me to go right home. By the time I got there, my father was dead. The tenement was crowded with friends and family. My mother sat silent beside my father, who lay on his bed, but she did not weep. It was my first sight of death. When I looked at my father, I remembered that earlier time when my mother was near to death; I remembered how her hand had looked. My father's face, and all that was visible of him, looked like that.

The rest of that day is a blur. Ladies sat in our parlor, sewing burial garments. People went to the station to meet my brothers, who were coming from New York, where they both had their first jobs. The lapel of my jacket was ripped, a fixed ritual of mourning. I must have gone to bed very late that night, but when I did, the house was still full of people. I lay in bed, half wakeful, and I missed the creak of my father's footsteps as he walked the kitchen floor invoking the four benevolent angels. I had long since got over my preoccupation with the Other, and I realized that now the four had also vanished, forever. I should thereafter know them only by name. The Malach Hamoves, his feat accomplished, must be off on other chores. Soon, in the elegiac, consolatory hum from the other room, I distinguished the voice of Myra Ellender. I found myself listening for Myra's voice, separating it from the medley of voices, and suddenly I began to long for Myra in a wholly new way. This longing was so violent that it was in itself shattering, but that it should assail me so nakedly now, of all times, when all my thoughts should have been stricken ones, devoted to my father alone, overcame me with a sense of guilt that was even more devastating than the other emotion. It was as if, with God's deputy gone forever from our house, a dreadful saturnalia had been released to ravage me obscenely.

By dint of patient maneuvering on the part of Willie Lavin, I was transferred, after two years at Clark, to Harvard, and after that I was never to live in Worcester again, for I spent the summers with my brothers in New York. After I left home, my mother went to live with one of her married sisters in another house on Providence Street, and when this sister died, her husband married again, and my mother stayed on with her brother-in-law and his new wife. This uncle by marriage was not lucky with his wives. My aunt's first successor left him because he wouldn't take her to the movies. My uncle thought the movies a sinful diversion; if he had any spare time, he spent it in the synagogue. He succeeded, however, in marrying a third lady, with less giddy proclivities, and my mother lived with them also.

When I was graduated from Harvard, I came to New York to try to find a job. It took me about six years to find even an unsteady one, and I spent most of my time writing plays, none of which I was able to sell. For a long time, in those early New York years, I had a recurrent dream: I was in Cambridge, it was spring, and I was lying on the grass by the Charles River, reading a novel. I would wake up morning after morning from this happy dream to find myself prospectless, in an unpromising city. I would be seized, when I was especially depressed, with an almost uncontrollable desire to see my mother. Sometimes I yielded to this impulse; at other times I mastered it. I felt in those moments that she was the only person in the world I wanted to talk to, although the Yiddish I had known when I was young had atrophied to such a degree that I could hardly say anything at all to her. I could not even write a note in Yiddish, so I would write to an uncle who read English to tell my mother I was coming to Worcester. Often I had a change of heart on the train; since there was no way of really communicating with my mother, the journey was pointless, and in any case I could not tell her that things were not well with me. Having written, though, there was no turning back, and before long I was walking into the yard of the tenement house where she lived and she was on the upstairs piazza waving to me.

Fortunately, my mother did not want to talk. She would simply ask how I was and how my brothers were and I would say "Fine," and she would busy herself at once making tea. Sometimes, in the earlier visits, I would fall into the old routine and follow her about the kitchen so closely as to discommode her movements. Then she would look over her shoulder at me and laugh memorially. Under my pursuit, she would accelerate her movements to escape me; she would flick strands of her hair from her forehead with a quick, helpless gesture, as if she were brushing off a fly, and I would hear again the muttered, familiar epithet. Once we had settled down with our cups of tea, she would sit at the table across from me. And then would come the inevitable questions that I dreaded: Why wasn't I married and when would I be? I could not have answered these questions even if I had had the vocabulary. I kept trying to tell her, in my few words of Yiddish, that the event was imminent. This did not satisfy her; she wished it to be instantaneous. After some years of these promises, she would remind me that I had made similar ones on my earlier visits. In time, she became more searching on this point. Since the event was imminent, who was the girl? I had to improvise prospects. Then would come inquiries about the girl's family, and I had to improvise whole sets of future in-laws.

Among the mothers of Providence Street, the wish to see their children married was almost a mania. To illustrate my mother's fixation on this score, I must mention the fact that, after many years of effort, I finally sold a play. It was produced in New York, and later a road company was sent out. It played a one-night stand in Worcester. I was not present, but, from what I heard, there must have been considerable ado about it on Providence Street, and the theatre must have been filled with my relatives. One of my uncles took my mother. His English was so sketchy that he could have followed very little of it; nevertheless, he was enthusiastic. My mother, who had understood none of it, was noncommittal. On the way home, my uncle pressed her for an opinion. She would not give one. "Tell me," she asked him, "why doesn't he get married?"

In November of 1944, I returned on the *Elizabeth* from a trip I had made to England. It had been a trying journey. The ship was bringing several thousand casualties back from the front; the other passengers, mostly journalists and civilian technicians, were crowded in, eight or ten to a cabin; the blare of the loudspeakers, giving instructions for abandon-ship drills and announcements of meals for such of the wounded as could go to the dining saloon, was unremitting; the portholes were blacked out; the decks were curtained with canvas; with the zigzag course the ship was forced to follow, the crossing took seven days. On the morning we were to land, I was up and walking the decks at five o'clock. It was exhilarating to do this now that one knew the waters were at last free of submarines. And although we were at war, I had an extraordinary sense, because of the English scene I had just left, of being at peace. It was a morning of lambent clarity—the rocks jutting from the water, the lighthouses, the uninhabited, casual islands that seemed to be cut out of the surface of the sea with a diamond edge. The air was sharp; it had none of the softness of the early morning when I had walked with my father to fetch Jim Nightingale, some forty years before. That walk came back to me then, and I compared this morning with that other one, which had become, for me, the matrix of all early mornings. I felt the old anxiety to see my mother, who had not been told that I had gone abroad. She was still living in Worcester, and I determined to go there to see her within the next few days. When I reached New York that afternoon, my brothers told me that she had died that morning. She had been taken to Saint Vincent's Hospital a few days earlier. She had asked to die.

The next afternoon, my brothers and I went to

Worcester. We were received at the funeral home by a squat man in a derby hat. He was dressed with truculent formality in striped trousers and a double-breasted business jacket. We went in to see my mother. She was calm. Her face did not have the anxious look one sees sometimes on the faces of the dead. Malach Hamoves, the Black Angel, had reached her at last, but since she had invited him, his touch had been gentle, even benign.

4

MR. LAVIN, MR. LUPKIN, AND
DR. ABERCROMBIE

For the Easterner on the Pacific Coast, the New York papers take on an alarming importance. They come three days late, but their arrival constitutes a rendezvous with whatever remains of one's past. I remember how, one Sunday in February, 1932, a New York paper led me to a more than ordinary rendezvous with my own past. I was in temporary exile in Hollywood that year, and that particular afternoon I had settled down happily with the New York *Times* of the preceding Thursday and was browsing contentedly through the obituary page. (From the West Coast, death in the East somehow always seems glamorous.) Almost immediately, I found myself involved with the *Times'* recapitulation of the career of a Massachusetts educator who had just died in Boston.

"D. W. ABERCROMBIE, EDUCATOR, IS DEAD," announced the headlines. "Principal Emeritus of Worcester Academy, Which He Headed from 1882 to 1918; Made Several Trips to Europe to Study Educational Systems; Published Many Articles." I went on to read the story of Dr. Abercrombie's career, but however laudable the *Times* made it out to seem, I took no joy in it. I became conscious almost at once of embarrassment and malaise, without at first having any idea of the cause. By the time I had finished the obit, I felt actually hot—I must have been blushing. When Dr. Abercrombie took charge of Worcester Academy, the article stated, it had only thirteen pupils. It now had over two hundred students and was one of the best-known preparatory schools in the state. This was admirable, but it made my embarrassment more painfully acute. By the time it was disclosed that Dr. Abercrombie's career, all in association with New England schools, had lasted for more than forty years and that he had made several visits to Europe to study educational systems, I felt myself perspiring faintly, and when it was further revealed that he had been sent, as an honorary representative of the United States Bureau of Education, to study methods in German secondary schools, I was so uncomfortable that I had to force myself to go on. In contemplating the details of Dr. Abercrombie's career, I had an increasingly horrid sense of intrusion, of a kind of obscene invasion of his privacy, and what made it even more awful was the overwhelming impression of recurrence. I seemed to have had the same experience before. Here I was, doing it again! I read every word: how many of Dr. Abercrombie's addresses on education had been published, in addition to articles on education and on school administration; how he was a native of Bolling Green, Macon County, Alabama; how he had got his A.B. from Harvard in 1876 and had remained in Cambridge an extra year to study law. I drank in his honorary degrees, his marriage, his children. I read it all and let the *Times* fall from my hands. I was trembling; I was hot with shame.

I asked myself why. And then there took place in my memory a "quick dissolve," a phrase I had used that very morning to convey a shift in intimacy between two characters in the moving picture I was working on. Suddenly I knew why. It had nothing to do with Dr. Abercrombie, really. It even had nothing to do with me, really, though it did me no good to tell myself so. It had to do with Mr. Lavin and Mr. Lupkin and a ride I happened to take with them on the Providence Street trolley car. I hadn't thought of Mr. Lavin or Mr. Lupkin for nearly forty years, but I remembered them now with mortifying clarity.

The Providence Street car was a kind of

Toonerville trolley which jerked slowly up the steep hill. It had benches along each side, and the aisle between them was very narrow. There was a cord, hanging from the ceiling and running the length of the car, which you pulled when you wanted the car to stop.

The trolley ride I remembered so painfully took place on a Friday afternoon. I found myself—I couldn't have been more than nine or ten years old—bumping up the hill in the crowded car, full of my older co-religionists going home to prepare for Friday-night synagogue service. I was sitting alongside the Messrs. Lavin and Lupkin. They were both well known in our community, partners in a clothing establishment. Mr. Lavin, the father of my mentor, Willie, was a big man, with a large face and coarse features and a grating voice; Mr. Lupkin was much smaller, with spectacles and an innocent, kindly look. Mr. Lavin was considered brilliant; certainly he was tremendously energetic and his activities went on till he died at a great age, in harness. Mr. Lupkin was considered rather stupid but amiable; he was commonly in a state of ecstatic acquiescence, bobbing his head and agreeing to everything. Often he would nod at you violently even before you required affirmation. There sat Mr. Lavin and Mr. Lupkin and there sat I, and across the narrow aisle from us, so close that his knees almost touched the bulky Mr. Lavin's, sat Dr. Daniel Webster Abercrombie.

I don't know now how I knew it was he, but I did. Perhaps he had been pointed out to me before, but anyway I knew him. I remember him vividly as he sat there; he was just under medium height, slim, almost frail, and in spite of his pince-nez and a black overcoat with black silk facings on the lapels, his manner was modest. There he sat, tightly ingested into the Jewish population of Worcester. He was looking off into space, his eyes fixed on some happy hunting ground of his own—a region, I sensed, where there were no foreigners. He was pretending, I was sure, that there were no Jews in the world. I remember feeling an intense self-consciousness. I hoped my elders would make a good impression on Dr. Abercrombie, exhibit to him a certain elegance of behavior. I don't know what I expected them to do, but I yearned to have them at least present a united front of suavity.

Whatever I hoped for, Mr. Lavin did precisely the reverse. He had been staring fixedly at Dr. Abercrombie, and to my horror, I saw him reach out and put his pudgy forefinger practically in the educator's face. This was not out of pugnacity; it was merely a gesture of identification for Mr. Lupkin's benefit. Mr. Lavin's guttural tones grated out over the whole car; since he knew little English, he spoke in Yiddish, but the precision of his gesture made the subject of his conversation unmistakable.

"You see that man?" he inquired of Mr. Lupkin.

Mr. Lupkin nodded eagerly. "I see him," he said.

"Surely I see him."

"That man," said Mr. Lavin impressively, "is Dr. Abercrombie, the president of the Academy."

Dr. Abercrombie—no longer able to pretend that he was alone in the world, for there was Mr. Lavin's fist before his face to refute him—fidgeted uneasily. He shifted his eyes to another point on the ceiling. As for me, I wanted (a little ahead of my time) to be vaporized, and I should have liked the Messrs. Lavin and Lupkin to accompany me.

For once, the eternally acquiescent Mr. Lupkin was skeptical. He stared at the squirming prexy. "That man Dr. Abercrombie?" he asked incredulously.

"That's Dr. Abercrombie," said Mr. Lavin positively.

I remember that I had a mute desire to explain to Dr. Abercrombie what was behind this vocal, public identification. For even at ten, I knew that in pointing out Dr. Abercrombie, Mr. Lavin's gesture was one of pride. An illiterate man himself, he worshipped, as did most of the occupants of that car, any form of education. For him, for them all, Dr. Abercrombie was the living embodiment of education. There, in their midst, education sat, paying a nickel fare like themselves, and they were awed and exalted. I deplored Mr. Lupkin's unbelief, but understood it, too. The fact is that, for Mr. Lupkin, the physical materialization of Dr. Abercrombie was rather a disillusionment. He simply couldn't imagine that such a little, unassuming man could be Dr. Abercrombie.

After allowing his eyes to run over Dr. Abercrombie's features, hat, pince-nez, and overcoat, Mr. Lupkin, for the first time in his life, made a positive assertion. "This," he said, as if he were referring to a specimen preserved in alcohol, "can *not* be Dr. Abercrombie!"

Mr. Lavin was furious. To be contradicted at all was irritating to his imperious nature and to be contradicted by his cowed partner was unprecedented. He was livid. "I tell you," he shouted, and his swerving fist narrowly missed Dr. Abercrombie's stomach, *"that's Abercrombie!"*

By this time, the attention of the whole car was focussed on the fascinating mystery; all eyes eagerly searched the putative Dr. Abercrombie for some final clue. But I could endure no more. Although it was long before my stop, I rose weakly to reach for the bell cord.

Lavin accosted me. "You speak English," he rasped. "Ask him is he Abercrombie or isn't he."

I was unable to speak. I was unable to do anything. Mr. Lavin was sarcastic. "What's the matter?" He glowered at me. "Have you gone dumb all of a sudden?"

I don't know what would have happened had not the Irish conductor come by at this moment for the fares. "How are you today, Dr. Abercrombie?" he inquired respectfully as he took the president's nickel.

Mr. Lavin, though he could not understand the conductor very well, at least recognized Dr. Abercrombie's name and turned on his companion with angry triumph. The mystery solved, the whole car relaxed.

"Well?" demanded Mr. Lavin bitterly of Mr. Lupkin. More accurately, he said, *"Nu!,"* which can be very declamatory. "Who knows Dr. Abercrombie better—you or me?"

His intimacy with the president established beyond peradventure, Mr. Lavin sat back, glowering. But Mr. Lupkin, defeated by the facts, could still not reconcile himself to them. He gave Dr. Abercrombie one final, dismissive stare and then made a gesture of a kind of despairful negation. It said plainly, "Well, if this is indeed Dr. Abercrombie, then anybody can be anybody."

For me, this contemptuous gesture of Mr. Lupkin's was the last turn of the screw, but I am sure Dr. Abercrombie did not see it. The moment he had got his change from the conductor, he had returned to the rapt contemplation of his private and homogeneous world on the ceiling. But I jumped off the car and ran as fast as I could up the steep hill toward home. I was hot all over. In fact, I am sure that not since have I blushed so comprehensively, or, at least, not till I read that obituary in the *Times* forty years later.

5

DEBS ON YOM KIPPUR

For us children, Yom Kippur, the Day of Atonement, was a tremendous event. We looked forward to it with a kind of morbid fascination. It meant a holiday from school, but it had no other festive connotation, and Yom Kippur Eve—*Erev Yom Kippur*—gave promise only of an interminable night and day of prayer and fasting for those of thirteen and over, and an acute intimation of doom for everybody. To us younger children, it seemed as if the purpose of the Day was to stave off, if possible, for one more year, by a twenty-four-hour assuagement of an implacable Deity, the incidence of all sorts of horrid fates. We believed that whether we would survive the next twelve months or not was definitely to be decided on this day of days. Thus the atmosphere of Yom Kippur Eve had all the tension of a murder trial at the moment when the jury comes back to announce its verdict. But we, of course, never got the verdict. We could only petition the Judge and hope for the best. Everything about the Day was awesome, and the ceremonies of its Eve, which began before sunset, were a fateful overture to the solemnities of the Day itself.

An hour or so before sunset—at which time the service in the synagogue across the street was to begin—my father would gather the family together for such propitiatory rites as could be performed at home. We would stand around him in a little semi-circle while he, intoning prayers in Hebrew, waved over his head, and ours, a live fowl. I did not then know that this rite was a pagan survival from a period now lost in the mists of antiquity, but I have learned since that a somewhat similar primitive religious practice survives among the Catholics in Haiti, where a cock is on certain occasions sacrificed to the Virgin Mary. On Providence Street, in my childhood, the bewildered bird was sacrificed only symbolically. It was preserved for its immolation on the following day, when it was served up at the dinner that broke the long fast of Yom Kippur. Our less orthodox Jewish neighbors waved coins about instead of live birds, and the money was later given to charity. A popular sum to use in the ritual, especially among the poor, was eighteen cents, because in Hebrew the letters that stand for "ten" and "eight," put together, mean "life," and thus were a strong nudge to the Lord in the direction of clemency. The attempt to beguile the Almighty with a pun was perhaps naïve, but it persisted. In our house, as I've said, we parried Fate with a fowl. It was borne in upon me at an early age that behind this symbolic, cabalistic ceremony was the idea that the Deity, in an absent-minded moment, might transfer the fate he had in store for one of us to the sacrificial bird, thereby reducing the potential family mortality in the forthcoming year by at least one. That such an escape was recognized as an outside chance, at the very best, is attested to by the fact that the ceremony didn't visibly cheer anybody up.

By sundown, all of Providence Street had gathered in the synagogue to remain until the evening ceremonies ended, two hours later. A few of the most devout stayed on through the night, praying, but the greater number went home to bed and returned the next morning at eight for the ceremonies of the Day itself, which continued until sunset. The fast for the adults was rigorous; not even a drop of water must pass the lips of the penitents from sunset till sunset. We children of less than thirteen did not have to keep the fast and most of us had another windfall—a recess at about eleven o'clock in the morning, during the half-hour prayer for the dead. It was forbidden for anyone whose parents were both still alive to be present during this prayer and, naturally, this gave the greater number of us youngsters an automatic respite. Any adults whose parents were living also left the synagogue at this time, but they stayed just outside, presumably meditating upon the mercy that excluded them from the building itself. We children, though, knew only that we had a half hour to ourselves, and sometimes we roamed far and wide, forgetting that we must be back the moment the prayer was over. It was, of course, mandatory that we be present for the rest of the day, especially during the mighty prayer that was, in a sense, the dramatic climax of the long service and expressed the essence of the occasion. This was the dread and beautiful *"Unsanneh Tokef Kedushas"* ("We Will Express the Mighty Holiness of This Day"). I can still hear its awesome Hebrew cadences. In unison the congregation introduced it:

> We will express the mighty holiness of this day, for it is one of awe and dread. Thereon is Thy dominion exalted and Thy throne is established in mercy, and Thou sittest thereon in truth. Verily, it is Thou alone who are judge and arbiter, who knowest all and art witness; Thou writest down and settest the seal. Thou recordest and tellest; yea, Thou rememberest the things forgotten. Thou unfoldest the records, and the deeds therein inscribed proclaim themselves; for lo! the seal of every man's hand is set thereto. The great trumpet is sounded;

the still small voice is heard; the angels are dismayed; fear and trembling seize hold of them as they proclaim: Behold the Day of Judgment! The host of heaven is to be arraigned in judgment. For in Thine eyes even they are not pure; and all who are about to enter the world dost Thou cause to pass before Thee as a flock of sheep.

For each member of the congregation this was a climactic personal prayer and everyone chanted it fervently, the cantor's voice sometimes rising above the others in awesome coloratura. The prayer continued:

As a shepherd seeks out his flock and causes them to pass beneath his crook, so dost Thou cause to pass and number every living soul, appointing the measure of every creature's life and decreeing his destiny.

On the first day of the year it is inscribed, and on the Day of Atonement the decree is sealed, how many shall pass away and how many shall be born; who shall live and who shall die, who at the measure of man's day and who before it; who shall perish by fire and who by water; who by the sword, who by wild beasts, who by hunger and who by thirst; who by earthquake and who by plague, who by strangling and who by stoning; who shall have rest and who shall go wandering, who shall be tranquil and who shall be harassed, who shall be at ease and who shall be afflicted; who shall become poor and who shall wax rich; who shall be brought low and who shall be exalted.

Before I even entered the synagogue, I began to visualize what was going on Above on the Day of Atonement: the All-Seeing, like a celestial Actuary, a kind of immense Mosaic statistician, graving prophetic casualties onto some vast double-entry ledger of stone, with a quill that was a gleaming and pointed pillar of quartz. The short walk across the street to the synagogue after the feeble ruse with the fowl was like a stroll across the Bridge of Sighs. Descending doom was already upon us; we did not know precisely what it was we had done or how we had sinned, but we knew that we had to pay for it. It was the vagueness of the mass guilt that gave it its special, terrorizing quality. For me, a macabre and scary detail of the general atmosphere was that my father, before he piloted the family across to the service, would put on an all-enveloping white robe called a *kittel*. All the other elders of the synagogue did the same. I learned very young that these robes were the shrouds prescribed by tradition for the final journey, and so exigent was the sense of the life-and-death verdicts to be recorded on this day that the mortuary costume seemed to me not at all unnatural.

For us younger children, there was, as I have said, an oasis in the desert of uninterrupted prayer, a delicious escape in the forenoon. Paradoxically, this interlude, for which we could hardly wait, was for our elders the most intimately felt and mournful of the whole day. It was called *Yizkor*—the Memorial for the Dead—and was a period of prayer for those against whom the Almighty had, in the past year or long since, made a punitive entry on his ledger. The younger element blessed the theologian who had made the ruling that excluded most of us. To be free for a space, and to escape awhile the awful weight of an adverse balance piling up against us in the Judgment Book was almost too good to be true. With the threnodies of our mourning elders echoing in our ears, we, the young and unbereaved, made joyously for the street.

Once we were outdoors, our sense of release was almost unbearable, and to work off some of our energy we always hurried off "down the line," as we called it, down the main street of town, in a parade of liberty. Down Providence Street hill we ran, past the Providence Street School, past the humble little rival synagogue, the Balbirishocker Schul. We heard its cantor singing from inside. His petition sounded ineffectual to us; we felt he could not possibly receive for his congregation the same favorable attention from the Celestial Scribe that ours did. We went on through Grafton to Front Street. In the winy October forenoon, with the air fermenting and mellowing in the warm sun, the vigilance of the Actuary seemed somehow relaxed, and the world was more intensely ours because we had lately been so confined. Yom Kippur did not decimate the pedestrian population of Worcester's streets, as it was said to do in New York. There were the usual people about, but they had the anemic, unzestful look of the unliberated. They walked Providence and Front Streets as if it were quite commonplace to be doing so. We were always mystified by their casualness.

On one of these occasions, when I was perhaps nine or ten years old, we had run down the hill and were walking happily and without objective on Front Street. We passed Horticultural Hall, a building we knew well because it was often hired for Providence Street weddings. Swinging adventurously around the corner into Main Street, we were soon abreast of the dark Corinthian facade of Mechanics' Hall. Now, Mechanics' Hall was a very different cup of tea from Horticultural Hall. It was august and forbidding, while Horticultural Hall was lightsome. You couldn't conceivably be married in Mechanics' Hall. It was reserved for the séances of the visiting great. (Later I was to hear there such virtuosi as Paderewski, Elman, William Jennings Bryan, and Theodore Roosevelt.) Ordinarily, it would never have occurred to us to broach this reserved interior, but as we approached it that morning, some rather forlorn-looking people were straggling in. A sophisticated and slightly older contemporary, Allie Price, scouted around among the stragglers and reported to us that "some feller Debs" was inside and was going to make a free speech. He was running for President and, for nothing, we could hear him speak. We joined the seemingly indifferent electorate and found our-selves in the dim, galleried auditorium. All alone on the platform sat a tall, gaunt, bald-headed man with a prominent, beaked nose. On the wall behind him hung three enormous oil paintings of frock-coated New England worthies, who appeared to be look-ing down with frigid disapproval at the candidate. The hall was immense, the audience tiny and scat-tered. At first, we boys sat timidly in the back. But as a few more unimpressive people wandered in and sat in the front rows, we also moved forward circumspectly, a row or two at a time, until, when Debs rose to speak, we were down under the plat-form and literally at the speaker's feet.

Though I cannot remember a single word that Debs said that morning to his apathetic audience and I never saw or heard him again, I am sure that this chance visit gave to all my later life an orienta-tion it would otherwise not have had—a bias in favor of those who had suffered from cruelty or cal-lousness. This was not because of any specific argu-ment or thought that I carried away from that meet-ing. It was simply because of the overwhelming impression that Debs' personality made on me. Most of all, I remember his intensity and what seemed to me to be his quivering sensitiveness to pain. The latter showed in his eyes, voice, and ges-tures. I remember his getting up and starting to speak. He wore a baggy, unpressed, cheap-looking gray sack suit, a shirt with a soft collar, and a black four-in-hand tie. As he began to talk, I was suddenly seized with a fear that we wouldn't get back to the synagogue in time to hear the *"Unsanneh Tokef,"* a lapse that would be simply unthinkable. The whole procedure—Debs' presence here as well as my own—seemed to me so grotesquely lacking in a sense of proportion as to verge on the insane. That Debs or anybody else could be troubling himself about as transitory a bauble as the Presidency of the United States when, only a mile or so away, an eternal and far greater decision was even then being held in the balance for or against him was only less remarkable for its bravado than that I myself, in that dread instant, could be sitting there listening to him. I felt that I must get up at once and hurry back to the synagogue. If Debs was foolhardy and wanted to run the risk, all right, but I couldn't be involved in so reckless a gamble. Nevertheless, I sat on there, torn between the attraction exercised by the man and the horrid necessity of getting back to the synagogue. There was something about Debs' delivery that I have never encountered since. He was tall and angular, and he leaned far over the edge of the platform, as if to get close to each one of his listeners. His arms reached out, as if to touch them. But what must have held me there was the growing conviction that he, too, was up against an antagonist, as powerful as the great Judge, and that the struggle here also was for life or death, that the issue was crucial and the hope of victory infinitesimal. On a different plane, the issue was as real as the issue on the hill, except that there, in the synagogue, the hope was in petition, whereas here there was some kind of struggle the scope and the intensity of which I could only feel, without in the least grasping it.

Oddly enough, on a much later Yom Kippur, when I was in my teens, I went into Mechanics' Hall to hear Woodrow Wilson, who was there on the same errand as Debs'. (People seemed always to be running for President on Yom Kippur.) On that later occasion, the visit was much less tense; I was already somewhat emancipated and I did not feel as I entered the hall that I was running the gantlet between two rows of avenging archangels. Wilson, I remember, was introduced by Dudley Field Malone, whose enthusiasm for his hero was so extravagant and rhetorical that when Wilson finally spoke, it seemed to me that he let his sponsor down grievously. Malone was so much the louder and funnier of the two that I wondered why he wasn't the candidate. The audience was as small as it had been for Debs. Wilson wore a gray business suit, just as Debs had, but Woodrow's coat and trousers had a sharp, Princetonian crease. With Debs, the issue—whatever it was—seemed to transcend the contest; Wilson's talk was confined to the contest, and he was so colorless that his chances of winning

it seemed laughably remote. Malone possibly;
Wilson certainly not. The fact is that Debs had
become for me the standard of reference, by which
his successors invariably suffered—even William
Jennings Bryan and Theodore Roosevelt, who
spoke at evening meetings to crowds that filled the
hall. But neither of these speakers seemed to be
engaged in a contest as formidable as the one
waged by Debs; they fulminated against gold and
tariffs and refractory Cabinet members, opponents
within the realm of the defeatable, and through all
their struggles they remained well fed and genial.
They were not stripped, as was Debs, of everything
but the spirit of humanity.

Debs finished. The little audience crowded forward to the platform to shake hands with him. I
had a last vision of him leaning down to receive the
congratulations of his listeners. They were smiling
and seemed happy, as if they had found a champion; the dejection I had noticed in the beginning had
disappeared. But by this time the terror of missing
the other Judgment, on Providence Street, had fall-
en heavily upon all of us truants, and we hurried up
the aisle and outdoors in a kind of panic.

We ran back to Providence Street at a dogtrot.
The sense of release we had felt when we left the
synagogue had vanished. From one crisis of life, we
had inadvertently stumbled into another, almost
equally stringent. I kept thinking of Debs. Of what
avail would his election be if at this moment the pil-

lar of quartz were scratching a fatal entry opposite his name? I passionately hoped it wasn't, but you never could tell. Certainly it was tactless of him to voice his grievances as if their removal would be merely the righting of a wrong, and not an act of mercy. What if Debs were to appear before the Actuary Himself? What if he were to intercede for someone marked to die by fire or by water? Was he not powerful enough and eloquent enough to win a reprieve, to placate or—blasphemous thought—perhaps even to defeat the great Judge? In the mighty ultimate contest, I felt a passionate enlistment on the side of Debs. As I think of it now, this was probably my first beginning rift of skepticism, my first faint doubts about the rigid theological beliefs of my forefathers.

But once we were inside the synagogue, Debs, as well as my momentary blasphemy, evaporated utterly. We had indeed missed the beginning of the crucial prayer. This was so black a sin that our hearts sank. Already the congregation, awed and self-absorbed, was chanting the inventory of its possible dooms—". . . who by hunger and who by thirst; who by earthquake and who by plague . . ." Terrified and out of breath from running, I stood at the back of the congregation and looked around for my father, praying that he had not seen me come in late. Thankfully, I spotted his robed figure in its accustomed place. He was bending over the prayer book on his reading desk and was too much absorbed to notice me. I breathed easier and relaxed a bit, trying to assume the nonchalant and habituated air of one who had never been outside at all and who had never, even for a single moment, abandoned his devotions.

Providence Street, circa 1895.
"I remember Providence Street best in the clear twilight of evenings in early summer. We boys had probably been for a swim at Jerry Daly's bath-house on Lake Quinsigamond. The long trudge back from the lake along Shrewsbury Street was easier than the walk to the lake; most of the four miles was downhill, for one thing...."
– S.N. Behrman.
(Photo, Picturesque Worcester, 1895)

Providence and Grafton Streets, circa 1895. *"Past the grade crossing on Grafton Street we were practically home; the short length of Grafton Street led into Grafton Square at the base of Providence Street hill."* – S.N. Behrman. (Photo, Picturesque Worcester, 1895)

31 Providence St. in the 1950's.
"We lived, when I was a child and until I left Worcester, in a triple-decker tenement a quarter way up the long hill that was Providence Street. The street belonged to a few Irish, to a few Poles, and to us.... They had balconies, front and back, which we called piazzas. The yards in the back had fruit trees.... My family, including my grandmother and two aunts, occupied three of the six flats at 31."
– S.N. Behrman.
(Photo reprinted with permission of the Worcester Telegram & Gazette)

#74 Providence Street, "the Wolfson mansion," as it looked in the 1950's. *"It was a house around which one could build dreams. . . . Mr. Wolfson's house, with its stained-glass window was the show place of Providence Street. . . . Providence Street always referred to Mr. Wolfson as the Gvirr. Gvirr was what we should now call tycoon. . . . The Wolfsons were the fir people on Providence Street to own car. It was a Winton Six."*
– S.N. Behrman.
(Photo courtesy of Oak Hill CDC)

The Wolfson mansion, 1911.
"But the magic and the wonder of Mr. Wolfson's mansion was that it had, instead of the customary parlor windows, with their lace curtains on brass rods, a great, darkly resplendent oval of stained glass. . . ."
– S.N. Behrman.
Closer inspection reveals the stained glass window not to be oval, but it is "resplendent" just the same.
(Photo from the collections of the Worcester Historical Museum, Worcester, Mass.)

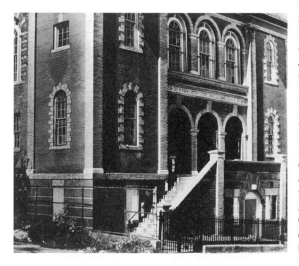

Shaarai Torah East, #32 Providence St
"The synagogue we attended was directly across the street from our flat so it was especially convenient in inclement weather. . . in 1906, when he (the Ramaz) was presiding over the Congregation Kehilath Jeshurun, on East Eighty-fifth Street, in New York. . . the Providence Street Synagogue. . . decided to pay him an architectural tribute by rebuilding the house of worship on Providence Stree in exact, if scaled-down imitation of t Ramaz's synagogue." – S.N. Behrman
(Photo by Daniel Farber, 1983, from the collections of the Worcester Historical Museum, Worcester, Mass.)

orcester Academy, circa 1900. *"A little below the Cromptons', across the street, was a lled town - a vast enclosure with fascinating, improbable, chocolate-colored turrets. This s the Worcester Academy.... The Academy was a private school which attracted dents from all over the United States - mythical young men who could pay for their condary educations."* – S.N. Behrman. (Photo, Fifty Glimpses of Worcester, 1900)

Worcester Academy baseball team, 1888, of the era remembered by Behrman. *"The members of the Worcester Academy baseball team were our childhood heroes.... We watched for e appearance of the Academy players on the Providence Street car, hung around the walled city of the Academy to catch a glimpse of them, and, fore their games, we were in a state of feverish excitement."* – S.N. Behrman. (Photo, courtesy of Worcester Academy)

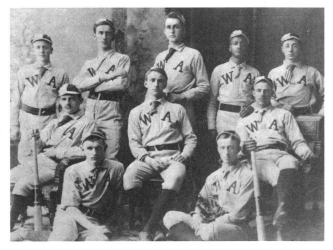

"There was one other great demesne at the top of the hill - St. Vincent's Hospital.... My mother was always being hospitalized in St. Vincent's and she died there. She never could say enough in praise of the nuns.... It was a charming consideration on the part of the nuns that they veiled the holy pictures on the walls - the Virgins and the Crucifixions - to spare the religious sensibilities of their orthodox Jewish patients." – S.N. Behrman. (1911 postcard, Abramoff collection)

"*As I look back on my school days in Worcester, in the Providence Street gra school at the start of the century, and later in the Classical High School, I ca see that these contemporary institutio were rather ineffectual in combatting t sombre fascination of the medievalism my home. There we were... a family uprooted from a veiled and ancient an unhappy past, and plumped down, un countably, in the tenement district of a industrial city in New England. The American myths I acquired in school h tory books... were thin and anemic co pared to the Biblical exploits I heard about at home.*" – S.N. Behrman.

▲ Providence Street School exterior, 1898.

➤ Providence Street School kindergarten students, 1902.

(Both photos from the collections of the Worcester Historical Museum, Worcester, Mass.)

Classical High School. (1909 postcard, Abramoff collection)

Poli's Theatre program. "*. . . She (Ida) attended the matinées at Poli's vaudeville theatre on Saturdays. Such a violation of the Sabbath was unthinkable. . . . One Saturday when a telegram arrived saying that Ida's mother was seriously ill, Harry went at once to Poli's and had Ida paged. When she was found, she pointed out that she had bought the ticket in advance, so that no money had changed hands on the sacred day.*" – S.N. Behrman. (Program, Abramoff collection)

Below: Poli's Theatre, exterior (1907 postcard, Abramoff collection)

Left: Worcester-made Osgood Bradley streetcar on the Providence St. line circa 1911 at the corner of Pleasant and Main Sts.

Right: An interior view of a similar car, 1913. "*The Providence Street car was a kind of Toonerville trolley which jerked slowly up the steep hill. . . . In the summer the Providence Street car was open; when it was crowded, as it generally was at about the time we would be walking home from the lake, we could hitch a ride on it easily.*" – S.N. Behrman. (Photos from the collections of the Worcester Historical Museum)

Worcester Public Library.
"A few streets down from Easton's was... the Worcester Public Library... an outlet to the universe.... The library had an enormous number of them (Alger books) and I devoured them; I used to take out one a day, swallow it, and return it the next day for another. They were heaven."
– S.N. Behrman.
(1906 postcard, Abramoff collection)

The "old" Union Station, circa 1901
"This station was very familiar to m principally because to satisfy an itch for travel, I had often boarded the incoming trains from Springfield or Boston and sat on the plush seats while the train stopped to take on Worcester passengers. I would get o at the last minute before departure, with the worldly air of one who has just completed a fatiguing journey."
– S.N. Behrman.
(Photo, The City of Worcester, Mass. ar Vicinity, 1901)

◄ Slater Building. *"When my pals on the Hill and I grew old enough to sniff emancipation, we used to walk boldly downtown to Main Street on Saturday mornings and ride up and down in the elevators of the Slater Building just for a fling at the illicit."* – S.N. Behrman.

► Bancroft Tower. *"I had an adventurous crony named Allie Price, who... had the startling idea... that he and I should sleep that night in Bancroft Tower... it is constructed solidly of New England granite.... Allie and I found that whatever you might do in Bancroft Tower, you couldn't sleep in it."*
– S.N. Behrman.

(Photo from the collections of the Worcester Historical Museum)

(1908 postcard, Abramoff collection)

Easton's Pharmacy.
"On Saturdays and holidays there was exaltation in going 'down the line' - the expression we used for going downtown. Past Elkind's, down Grafton, down Front, past the Common with its statue of the great Massachusetts Senator, George Frisbie Hoar; past the City Hall, to Easton's, at Main and Pleasant.... Easton's was the center of the world." – S.N. Behrman.
(Postcard, Abramoff collection)

Mechanics Hall.
"On Main St. was the gloomy cavern of Mechanics Hall, where Presidents spoke and great artists performed.... It was reserved for *the séances of the visiting great. (Later I was to* *hear there such virtuosi as Paderewski, Elman, William Jennings Bryan, and Theodore Roosevelt.)"* – S.N. Behrman. (1908 postcard, Abramoff collection)

White City on Lake Quinsigamond.
"Across the Lake, the water mirrored resplendently the dazzling lights of the amusement park, White City, with its Ferris wheel, chute-the-chutes, and penny peep shows...." – S.N. Behrman. (1906 postcard, Abramoff collection)

Lake Quinsigamond was a lovely lake - or so it seemed to us then - four miles long, dotted with islands, about four miles distant from the triple-decker tenement houses of Providence Street. In summer we boys went to sleep at night dreaming of the Lake and of the moment when we would arrive the next morning." – S.N. Behrman.
(1910 postcard, Abramoff collection)

Maureen Stapleton matchmaking as Ida in the 1958 New York production of *"The Cold Wind and the Warm."* The author's description in **The Worcester Account** of Ida: *"She looked down on professional matchmakers .... Ida had the true amateur's love, a devotion untainted by the profit motive. No one was safe from Ida - not even her own children, or any widowed in-laws, or her father."* (Photo by Fred Fehl)

rovidence Street" scene from the production of *"The Cold Wind and the Warm,"* at New
rk's Morosco Theatre, 1958. Left to right are Morris Carnovsky as Mr. Sacher; Suzanne
eshette as Leah; Timmy Everett as Tobey, the character based on Sam Behrman; and Eli
allach as Willie, based on Behrman's friend, Dan Asher. (Photo by Fred Fehl)

MOROSCO THEATRE

PREMIERE PERFORMANCE, DECEMBER 8, 1958

THE PRODUCERS THEATRE PRESENTS

A ROBERT WHITEHEAD PRODUCTION

ELI   MAUREEN
WALLACH   STAPLETON

THE COLD WIND AND THE WARM
by S. N. BEHRMAN

suggested by his "New Yorker" series
and book "The Worcester Account"

SANFORD MEISNER

MORRIS CARNOVSKY   SIG ARNO

TIMMY EVERETT   CAROL GRACE   SUZANNE PLESHETTE

Sidney Armus   Vincent Gardenia   Jada Rowland   Peter Trytler

Directed by
HAROLD CLURMAN

Settings by   *Costumes by*   *Lighting by*
BORIS ARONSON   MOTLEY   FEDER

Cast

(In order of appearance)

Tobey	TIMMY EVERETT
Willie	ELI WALLACH
Jim Nightingale	VINCENT GARDENIA
Ida	MAUREEN STAPLETON
Ren	JADA ROWLAND
Myra	CAROL GRACE
Aaron	PETER TRYTLER
Rappaport	SIG ARNO
Mr. Sacher	MORRIS CARNOVSKY
Dan	SIDNEY ARMUS
Leah	SUZANNE PLESHETTE
Norbert Mandel	SANFORD MEISNER

David Behrman of New York City, Sam and Elza's son, is a noted composer, musician and designer of music software. *"It was hard to escape the arts in our family."* Of his father, he recalls, *"We had an unusually close father-son relationship."*
(Photograph by Terri Hanlon)

Elza and Sam Behrman in Paris, 1952, in a photo taken by their only child, David, at age 15. The Behrmans wed in 1936; David was born the following year. Elza Heifetz Behrman had two children, Harold Stone and Barbara Gelb, from her previous marriage; she is the sister of the violinist Jascha Heifetz.
(Photo courtesy of David Behrman)

Dan Asher, Behrman's inseparable Worcester friend and the model for Willy Lavin. *"Willie was the best friend I have ever had, and his death many years ago was the greatest loss I had ever suffered.... During all these years there was no intellectual problem, no practical dilemma, no psychological crisis at home that I did not dump in Willie's lap. He became, so to say, my liaison officer between the medievalism of our household and the latter-day world...."*
– S.N. Behrman. (Photo courtesy of David Behrman)

SAMUEL NATHANIEL BEHRMAN

Born June 9, 1893, at Worcester, Massachusetts. Home address, 31 Providence Street, Worcester, Massachusetts. Prepared at Classical High School. At Clark College for two years. Price Greenleaf Aid; Elnathan Pratt Scholarship. Menorah Society.

S.N. Behrman from 1916 Harvard Class Album.
"After I had been at Clark for two years, Willie began to read about George Pierce Baker and his new Drama Workshop at Harvard, which was then much in the news.... The transfer from Clark was difficult, but Willie arranged it and I moved to Cambridge for my junior and senior years." – S.N. Behrman. (Photo courtesy of the Harvard University Archives)

S.N. Behrman in Salzburg, 1937, on the day his son, David, was born.
(Photograph by John Phillips)

Zelda Behrman, the author's mother, circa 1938. *"I wa[s] closer to my mother, and had an adoration for her that I never felt for my father.... She had blue eyes and soft brown hair.... I believe I was the only one in the famil[y] with whom she had a relationship that, in its sunniest moments, might be described as gay. I could make her laugh, and she came to expect me to."*
– S.N. Behrman.
(Photo courtesy of Marian Behrman)

Right: Inscriptions in the Behrman family "Shemot" or Torah. Note Joseph "Berman," the author's father, and the Water St. address, where the family first lived. Water Street was the retail heart of Worcester's immigrant Jewish neighborhood. (Photo courtesy of Elizabeth Behrman)

Left: Hebrew wording from the Behrman family Shemot which reads: "My dear father a[nd] teacher Joseph... died in the week of the Lord portion Vayechi, the sixth day of Tevet 5673 (Dec. 16, 1912).... May his soul be bound up in the Bond of life.... City of Worcester...."
(Photo courtesy of Elizabeth Behrman)

S.N. Behrman from Harvard 1916
Class 25th Anniversary Report.
(Photo courtesy of Harvard
University Archives)

This photo of Behrman, taken in 1952, accompanied the Associated Press obituary after his death on September 9, 1973.
(Photo, reprinted with permission from Clark University)

Behrman wrote the initial drafts of all of his books, plays, short stories and movie scripts in longhand. This is an early draft from "Malach Hamoves" and is similar to the first paragraph of that story, which is Chapter 3 of *The Worcester Account*.
(Photo courtesy of David Behrman)

"The Ramaz, who was then presiding over the Baldwin Place Synagogue, in Boston, traced his descent from a celebrated rabbi known as the Rashi, one of the greatest Talmudic commentators, who lived in France in the eleventh century." – S.N. Behrman.
(Photo courtesy of Rabbi Haskell Lookstein, Congregation Kehilath Jeshurun, New York, N.Y.)

a, the daughter of the Ramaz. *"When Ida, who was then seventeen, married my Uncle Harry, who was ten years older, she was a autiful girl, with large, clear blue eyes and bundant light hair.... Ida brought into our rather lugubrious, God-obsessed circle an xhilarating earthy gusto, strongly flavored with an almost ribald skepticism.... Her iety was more than merely paradoxical; it was downright shocking."*
— S.N. Behrman.
(Photo courtesy of Golda Weiss)

e Ramaz, circa 1920.
.. my Uncle Harry had made a emendous short cut to a vast a of learning when he married a, the daughter of the Ramaz, o was a world-famous rabbi."
S.N. Behrman. (Photo courtesy Golda Weiss)

The Ramaz. *"He was so famous that he was called not by his real name - Rabbi Moshe Zevulon Margolies - but by a name coined from his initials. The Ramaz looked like Moses, except that he wore gold-rimmed spectacles."* – S.N. Behrman.
(Photo courtesy of Rabbi Haskell Lookstein, Congregation Kehilath Jeshurun, New York, N.Y.)

Ida's daughter, Mrs. Gertrude Bergman, 1945. *"The daughter, nicknamed Go-Go had... some of Ida's effervescence. This was Ida's explanation of why Go-Go, unlike her two sisters, had not remained in Worcester but had married a New Yorker."* – S.N. Behrman.
(Newspaper clipping courtesy of Golda Weiss)

Ida and Newman of Newark (at right), with unidentified others in the 1920's. *"Newman was a tall, corpulent, imposing man with a small, trim, pointed white beard.... He was pious and he adored the Ramaz. When Newman met Ida, who by then was fifty years old... he fell in love with her at once...."* – S.N. Behrman.
(Photo courtesy of Golda Weiss)

Ida and her daughter Ann Feingold in swimsuits, and Ann alone; both photos circa 1920.
(Photos courtesy of Golda Weiss)

6

DAUGHTER OF THE RAMAZ

About the time I was born, there suddenly fell into my family's collective lap an unbelievable and breathtaking bounty. It had the quality of a miracle because it was so easy and instantaneous and transforming. It lifted my parents to the Providence Street skies, distinguished them. It was as if there had suddenly been conferred on my family—without any of its members doing anything at all to deserve it—the award of the Légion d'Honneur. From that moment, they were set apart, revered, envied. My father was highly thought of as a learned man, but the rest of us were ordinary enough. Why were we singled out for this extraordinary blessing? There were other learned men on the street, and *they* had families, too. Nevertheless, it was to us that it happened—the sudden arrival of a tremendous, unearned social increment—and nothing could be done about it by those who envied us. There was compensation even for them, because the lustre of our new distinction was great enough to shed its glow over the whole community. Had it been aware, all of Worcester might have revelled in it. But Providence Street knew, even if the rest of Worcester didn't. What happened was the totally unexpected engagement, in 1893, of my Uncle Harry, who lived a couple of blocks away on Providence Street, to a Boston girl named Ida, the daughter of the Ramaz.

There is an enchanting, almost untranslatable Yiddish play by Peretz Hirschbein called "Green Fields." It is laid in an impoverished ghetto village in Russia toward the end of the last century, and it tells of a wandering Talmudic scholar who is travelling on foot from a small Yeshiva, or rabbinical school, to a large, famous one in a big town hundreds of miles distant. He spends the night in the poor little hamlet. The illiterate Jewish peasant into whose yard he wanders is dazzled by the appearance of a man of the written word, and runs in to tell his family of the incredible stroke of good fortune. He is hysterical with gratitude to God. When the rich man of the village hears that the Talmudic scholar is staying in the poor man's house, he is angry. If this man of God is staying in the village,

naturally he must stay with him. The play is concerned with the fierce social rivalry in the village
over entertaining the poor scholar, over having as a
guest, if only for a few hours, a man who can read.
When I saw this play in Los Angeles some years
ago, performed with remarkable delicacy by Jacob
Ben-Ami, I understood better the sensation on
Providence Street when my Uncle Harry's engagement to Ida was announced. For Ida's father, the
Ramaz, was one of the most famous rabbis in the
world. He was so famous that he was called not by
his real name—Rabbi Moshe Zevulon Margolies—
but by a name coined from his initials. The Ramaz
looked like Moses, except that he wore gold-
rimmed spectacles. My family knew his face even
before the windfall, because his photograph hung in
the living room of our tenement, as it did in the living rooms of most other Providence Street tenements.

The Ramaz, who was then presiding over the
Baldwin Place Synagogue, in Boston, to which he
had been summoned from Lithuania seven years
before, traced his descent from a celebrated rabbi
known as the Rashi, one of the greatest of Talmudic
commentators, who lived in France in the eleventh
century. "Rashi" is also a name coined from initials;
his true name was Rabbi Shlomo Yitzhaki. (The
renowned Maimonides, whose full name was Rabbi
Moshe ben Maimon, was called the Rambam.) The
Rashi wrote one of the books of commentary—the

book, too, is known as the Rashi—that orthodox Jews labor over endlessly in their Talmudic studies. Modern French philologists, the encyclopedias say, still go to the Rashi for examples of French literary usage in the Middle Ages. Some notion of the Ramaz's vast influence may be gleaned from the fact that in 1906, when he was presiding over the Congregation Kehilath Jeshurun, on East Eighty-fifth Street, in New York—and he was still presiding over it when he died in 1936, at the age of eighty-five—a delegation of seventeen members of the Providence Street Synagogue, after visiting him to ask his advice on some synagogue question, decided to pay him an architectural tribute by rebuilding the house of worship on Providence Street in exact, if scaled-down, imitation of the Ramaz's synagogue.

The addition to the family of this illustrious aunt was a blessing far beyond what anyone could have imagined when the first breathless rumor of my Uncle Harry's engagement reached Worcester. Ida brought into our rather lugubrious, God-obsessed circle an exhilarating earthy gusto, strongly flavored with an almost ribald skepticism. The descendant of the Rashi bore her immense heritage lightly. Her gaiety was more than merely paradoxical; it was downright shocking. Whispers about Ida began to trickle along Providence Street soon after she settled down to housekeeping there with my Uncle Harry. In Worcester, Ida's attitude was always

118

that of a worldling forced by awkward circumstances to reside briefly in the provinces, and she sailed serenely above the invidious rumors. When Ida, who was then seventeen, married my Uncle Harry, who was ten years older, she was a beautiful girl, with large, clear blue eyes and abundant light hair; she looked like a Holbein. Men stopped to chat with her on the sidewalk. On Providence Street, this was not considered proper for a married woman. For a married woman whose father was the Ramaz, it was considered blasphemous. Uncle Harry's sister, a strict doctrinaire, complained to him that Ida's promiscuous sidewalk conversations were becoming a scandal. My uncle, still incredulous at the acquisition of such a bride, told his sister that it was none of her business and that the daughter of the Ramaz could do no wrong, and suggested that the reason she herself never became involved in sidewalk conversations was that she was aggressively homely. There were other charges against Ida. One was that she brought home too many bundles, by which people meant that she was extravagant and wasted her husband's substance. As my Uncle Harry was a peddler of notions—pins, needles, and other small household accommodations, which he sold from house to house in such outlying communities as Ware, Fitchburg, Auburn, Webster, and Shrewsbury—there couldn't have been too much substance to waste, but the charge persisted. Later on, Ida bought an upright piano, on time. This was a nine days' wonder. It wasn't that Ida was musical; she had discovered that her husband had a tendency to throw things around when he was irritated, and the solidity of a piano appealed to her. A more serious charge was that she attended the matinées at Poli's vaudeville theatre on Saturdays. Such a violation of the Sabbath was unthinkable. Harry fiercely denied the charge, but one Saturday when a telegram arrived saying that Ida's mother was seriously ill, Harry went at once to Poli's and had Ida paged. When she was found, she pointed out that she had bought the ticket in advance, so that no money had changed hands on the sacred day.

Ida always said that she was not a "private woman." Aware of the gossip about her, she explained that she simply had to talk to men on the sidewalk. By not being a "private woman" she meant that she was the helpless victim of that consuming interest in matchmaking which colored her entire life. This obsession Ida lovingly referred to as a disease; when it had begun she couldn't remember. She looked down on professional matchmakers, although she often had to come into contact with them, and, being proud of her amateur standing, she never took out a license. Ida had the true amateur's love, a devotion untainted by the profit motive. No one was safe from Ida—not even her own children, or any widowed in-laws, or her father. The feeling among orthodox Jews that a rabbi should not remain unmarried was a help to

Ida, for the Ramaz outlived three wives and gave her talents a lot of play.

From the beginning, Ida's career was dramatic, even lurid. Her marriage to my Uncle Harry, which took place in Meinhard Hall, in Boston, received more than the conventional reporting in the social columns, because most of the two thousand guests, as well as the bride, were poisoned. In Worcester, the event was known for years as Ida's Poisoned Wedding. "BEAUTIFUL BLONDE IN A BLUE SATIN DRESS POISONED AT HER OWN WEDDING," went one headline, and another declared, "RABBI'S DAUGHTER AND TWO THOUSAND GUESTS POISONED BY DEJECTED LOVER." The dejected lover was Perrele Greenbaum. Perrele had everything; he was successful in business, lively, generous, and very much in love with Ida. But he was a materialist and couldn't resist the Saturday influx of business at his store. He was so relaxed in religious matters that he even carried an umbrella on Saturdays. Because Ida was the daughter of the rabbi of the Baldwin Place Synagogue, the spiritual leader of Boston's orthodox Jewry, it was out of the question for her to marry him. Later, Ida always said that she decided, with a great effort, to be cool toward Perrele. To be cool toward such a man as Perrele taxed all her resources. The arrival of my Uncle Harry in her field of action posed a piquant technical problem, and its solution furnished an anodyne for her emotional troubles. Ida had already begun to dabble in matchmaking, and Harry went to see her to reconnoitre a possible bride. When Harry arrived to get the prospect's address, Ida noticed—she said later—that he was tall and very handsome, and wore a blue serge suit, but that he looked like a farmer. Yet she saw in Harry's eyes an expression that said, "Why do I go hence to search when here before me is beauty and at the same time the daughter of the Ramaz?" She also saw that he would never dare to ask for her hand—that he was too shy. Perrele came to take her for a walk in the park. Not trusting herself to continue cool toward him without some artificial aid, she said, "I bet you five dollars I can take that big farmer from Worcester away from the Boston girl." Perrele grimly accepted the bet. The news of the wager reached Uncle Harry, and he was emboldened to propose to Ida. Ida, feeling that her ability to remain cool to Perrele could not last indefinitely, accepted Uncle Harry on the spot. The theory was that the vindictiveness of the rejected Perrele lay behind the poisoned wedding. A newspaper reporter put the question to her flatly: Was it a rejected lover who had poisoned the wedding guests? Ida replied that she had no lovers; she had sweethearts—plenty—but they were all gentlemen and not poisoners of innocent people. The explanation of the poisoning was, in fact, much less romantic and far more sinister.

The events of the wedding day and the night

that followed it were always a nightmare to Ida. In her later years, she became very superstitious, and she attributed the misadventure at her wedding to the fact that it took place on the thirteenth of the month. When she was asked why she chose a notoriously unlucky day, she said, "I was a greenhorn then. In those days I was so ignorant I didn't know enough to be superstitious." An hour or so before the ceremony, an image of Perrele rose in her mind, and she decided that she couldn't go through with the wedding and that she must run away. But the wedding had been announced from the pulpit in the Baldwin Place Synagogue, and, in addition to the invited guests, several hundred uninvited people had shown up. It was pointed out to Ida that she couldn't disappoint so many people and that it would damage the good name of the Ramaz. She yielded to the principle of noblesse oblige. As she was standing under the wedding canopy, a visitation came to her: a voice like an angel's whispered, "Don't sit at the head table and don't eat!" This injunction she did not obey. Presently, there was panic in the hall and Ida understood why the voice had whispered to her. The guests all became very ill, those at the head table experiencing the first paroxysms; she became very ill herself. The Ramaz spoke to the guests quietly. The guilty ones would be discovered, he said, and God would punish them.

The Ramaz's prediction came true soon enough. The very next day, while the two thousand guests were still writhing, the wife of a butcher who had wanted to supply the meat for the wedding but who had been refused came rushing to the Ramaz crying hysterically. Her small son had just fallen off a roof, and she took this as a punishment from God. The Ramaz had turned this particular butcher down because he did not consider that his product met the ritual requirements for kosher meat. The Ramaz had many enemies among the Boston butchers, who found he could not be bribed to give certificates, or *Hashgohes*, qualifying their meat. The turndown for this big wedding was more than they could take. Some of the illegal butchers got together and raised fifteen hundred dollars, with which they bribed a druggist to concoct a poison that would not be fatal but would make the guests violently ill. When the plot was revealed by the butcher's hysterical wife, the Ramaz, instead of demanding that the offenders be sent to jail, rushed off to see the injured child, and this convinced the mother that the boy would get well, which, indeed, he did. God, said the Ramaz, would punish the plotters; revenge was not his province. So it came to pass. The druggist, who had been prosperous, gradually lost his business as the news got around; the illegal butchers and their leader, since the Ramaz continued to refuse to give them *Hashgohes*, were forced eventually to seek other trades. But the agitation caused by the poisoning was so great that Ida felt she couldn't go with her bridegroom on a honeymoon. They merely went home to Worcester instead, and Ida always insisted that Worcester was no place for a honeymoon.

Like her father, Ida was incapable of harboring grudges. Several years later, she ran into the guilty druggist in Grafton Square, in Worcester. He was down-and-out. He had been unable to re-establish himself in the drug business. Moreover, the girl he was going to marry had broken the engagement. The news of this shattered romance touched Ida. She did not offer, as she would have done for almost anyone else, to find him another girl, but she did say that if he needed a few dollars he might vaccinate her small son, the first-born of a family that included three daughters. He accepted the offer with gratitude. Ida took him home, and gave him some of the food for which she was by then famous and five dollars for the vaccination. Unfortunately, my Uncle Harry, when he got home, did not feel the same sympathy for the druggist. That Ida should permit an established poisoner to vaccinate their only son seemed to him beyond the bounds of tolerance. He had got over some of his bedazzlement at having acquired Ida, and he expressed his irritation in his usual way. He broke all the dishes in the house. He then stormed out, predicting that, thanks to Ida, their son would fall victim to all the diseases under Heaven. In later years, Ida, recalling the incident to her son with demure triumph, said that his father had been quite wrong; the druggist had done a very good job. "You had no diphtheria, no scarlet fever, no smallpox, no typhoid fever—only a little bit chicken pox," she said.

One reason Ida never really cottoned to Worcester was the absence of public benches there. She preferred New York because it offered a profusion of benches—on upper Broadway, in the parks, and, above all, in the lobbies of apartment buildings. It was as if a Parisian suddenly transplanted to Worcester were to find it arid because of the scarcity of sidewalk cafés. Some of Ida's most brilliant matches had their origin in chatty friendships formed while she was taking her ease on assorted benches in New York, which she often visited after her father moved there from Boston and where she went to live after my Uncle Harry died of pneumonia in 1915. From the bench in the lobby of her father's apartment house she hunted wives and husbands for lonely young people languishing in Worcester and its neighboring towns. She would say to visitors who came up to her father's apartment to sample her wonderful cooking, "Did you sit on the bench downstairs? What's doing there? Did you talk to anybody? Is there any news?" Frequently, after Uncle Harry died, she met men on benches who appealed to her and to whom she appealed; she might have married several of them, but there was sure to be a prospect on her list whose urge to marry was so insistent that she could not resist doing everything in her power to shift the focus to the client. Avocational considerations always came first with Ida. When she was living in New York, she often went back to Worcester to see two of her married daughters—all four of the children eventually married—but invariably she was impatient to return to her beloved benches. Once, it was suggested to her by a chauvinistic Worcesterite that, after all, there was always the chair on the back porch. She was contemptuous. "And who will I talk to on the back porch?" she demanded. "Who goes *by* a back porch? Who will I converse with? The bears in the back yard, maybe?" Ida insisted that on her very first evening in Worcester she had seen a bear on South Street. She was told it was probably a big black dog, but she was convinced it was a bear. This caused a trauma about Worcester from which she never fully recovered.

When one of her married daughters came to New York to visit her, Ida told her about a gentleman she had met on a bench on Central Park West the night before. He was an agreeable and elegant Long Islander who carried a cane—a mark of distinction to Ida—and he could be found on this bench every evening at eleven when he was in town. Ida wanted her daughter to meet him, so after an evening at the movies they went to the bench. When he appeared, Ida introduced her daughter and stated that she was married but had several

unmarried friends in Worcester who were cyno-
sures, compendia of all the graces. Conversation
was not the elegant Long Islander's long suit; Ida
had to do most of the talking. At one in the morning, Ida's daughter said that she simply had to go to
bed. "Can you understand the younger generation?" Ida demanded of the cane-carrier. "One
o'clock only and she wants to go to bed! Please, let's
stay awhile." The daughter wanted to know what
there was to stay *for*. "Who knows?" said Ida preg-
nantly. "People are still walking."

At the time Ida died, in 1946, her children discovered that during the last years of her life she had
occupied an official position she never told them
about. After the funeral, an elderly woman said to
them, "All the club members were at your mother's
funeral."

"I didn't know that Mother belonged to a club,"
one of the daughters said.

"But she did," said the mourner, rather testily. "It
was the club of all the women who sit on the benches of Broadway. Your mother was the President."

In general, Ida was happy in Worcester. She
indulged her hobby as well as she could in a community deficient in benches, and one time
Worcester rallied to her when New York had failed.
This incident was a beautiful manifestation of the
power and immortality of the legend of the Holy

Grail. Ida's nature was a fascinating mixture of down-to-earth contemporary realism and medieval mysticism; she adduced the episode of a girl named Felice and the apple as a prime example of the intervention of Divine Providence in her affairs. Uncle Harry always left Worcester early on Monday morning and was away until Friday evening, peddling notions in the surrounding towns. One day, in Fitchburg, he went to what Ida described as a "fashionable restaurant" for dinner. The widow who owned the restaurant had a daughter named Felice, who was, Ida admitted, "a little of a bookkeeper on the side." Ida did not wish her to be entirely a bookkeeper, because that would have seemed prosaic. Harry, pleased with his dinner, started chatting with the widow. "Where in Russia do you come from?" he asked, ruling out the possibility that she might have come from another country. She said that she was originally a Kroza girl, and Harry was delighted; as it happened, he said, he had married a Kroza girl.

"Who did you marry?" asked the widow.

"I married the daughter of the Ramaz," said Harry, trying to sound casual. The widow was stunned; when finally she believed the staggering truth, she ran to get Felice, so that the girl might behold with her own eyes the son-in-law of the Ramaz. She sent an effusive message to Ida, of whose deft matchmaking she had already heard, and she pressed into Harry's hand a photograph of

Felice for Ida's gallery. When Ida saw Felice's photograph, she melted, she said, because the girl was so beautiful. But, being rushed at the time, she did nothing about her.

Several years passed and Felice's mother died. One Friday when Harry came back from the road, he said Felice was lonely in Fitchburg without her mother, and implored Ida to find a husband for her. Ida could understand, although she had never been in Fitchburg, how lonely one could get there. For every bear roaming the streets in Worcester, she hazarded, there must be six in Fitchburg. But even a beautiful girl like Felice, she said flatly, could not, being a penniless orphan, expect to find a Galahad in Worcester. The Worcester men, she went on, were all fools. To find a husband for a girl like Felice, she must journey to the greener pastures of New York. A few evenings on the bench in the lobby of the Ramaz's apartment building or on one along upper Broadway, and Felice's destiny would be happily sealed. This plan seemed too informal to Harry; he feared Ida's absent-mindedness among the blandishments of New York. Time, he pointed out, was all-important. "In that case," said Ida, "I will go to see Levine, the professional matchmaker from the Bronx, and come right back."

Ida took Felice's photograph to New York. Levine, ordinarily an unemotional man, who handled his affairs with commercial detachment, was so impressed that, as Ida enthusiastically recounted on her return, "he right away melted also." Ida had never seen Levine melt before. Felice was something quite special, Levine admitted. That she was an orphan was not a total disadvantage; that she was penniless was more serious. Yet he was in correspondence at that very moment with a young man in Atlanta to whom money did not matter, since he had so much of his own. He was in the fur business, had an automobile, and was so artistic that he had recently had his ample apartment done over by an "interior man." Levine dispatched Felice's photograph to Atlanta, with documentation supplied by Ida, and waited confidently for results. They came. Levine's letter to Worcester, a week after Ida's return, reported ecstasy in Atlanta. Loneliness in Fitchburg was about to be assuaged. The young man in Atlanta wrote to Felice enclosing *his* photograph. Harry brought it from Fitchburg for Ida's inspection. The young man, said Ida, looked promising, except that he had no neck. His head seemed to emerge directly from his padded shoulders. She preferred a young man with a neck, but then penniless orphans from Fitchburg could not be choosy. It was, Ida stated, all settled.

After some correspondence between Felice and the wealthy aesthete from Atlanta, he promised to come to Fitchburg for a meeting. Ida was afraid that Fitchburg might depress him, and she invited Felice to come and stay with her in Worcester, so that she would have a more metropolitan background. Ida was sure that Felice's "connection" with her would not fail to impress the young man, although Levine had told her that the furrier was a reformed Jew and hardly ever went to the synagogue except during the high holidays. The meeting was set for a Sunday. On Thursday, Ida's son, then nine, woke up too ill, he insisted, to go to school. He demanded an apple. An apple, he cried, was the only thing that could drive away his illness. Ida searched the flat. There was always a barrel of apples on the porch, but today the barrel was empty. The invalid set up a howl. Ida was frantic. At this exigent moment, the postman arrived with a special-delivery letter. It was from Levine, who was full of apologies. A cautious man, he had sent to Atlanta, together with Felice's photograph, a photograph of one of his Bronx clients. The photograph of the Bronx girl had appealed to his Atlanta correspondent less than Felice's—about this, he begged Ida to believe, there could be no question—but the Bronx girl, unfortunately, had a well-off mother. This mother had suddenly felt called upon to offer her daughter the broadening advantages of travel. On the way South, mother and daughter had stopped off in Atlanta, and, oddly, in that warm climate, the mother had felt impelled to buy some furs for her daughter and herself. The tactile had triumphed over the ethereally photographic; the Bronx girl and the furrier were engaged. Levine was returning Felice's photograph, but he begged Ida to believe, again, that he would

132

keep her in mind, and he had no doubt that for so charming a girl, and with God's help, in the not too far distant future . . . Ida could not bear to read the hypocritical phrases; she threw the letter and the photograph to the floor. Had Levine been there, she admitted later, her blue eyes tranquil then and full of loving-kindness, she would have torn him limb from limb. She stood wondering how to break the awful news to Harry and Felice, and consumed with a desire to dismember Levine. To toy with an orphan's destiny! The treachery of sending off the extra photograph! And all the time, it finally penetrated her numbed and whirling senses, her little darling was screaming for an apple. It was at this very moment that there occurred what she could describe only as an act of God. It took the odd form of the voice of Ginsburg the peddler crying in the street outside, "Apples! Apples! Apples!" Ida ran to the window and called down to Ginsburg to bring up a peck. Now, Ida didn't like Ginsburg. She didn't like his looks. Theretofore, she said, she had never bought so much as an onion from him. But this was a crisis. First of all, she had to cure her boy and get him off to school; then she had to think more calmly about the disaster that had befallen Felice, who was even then preparing to come to Worcester to meet the faithless groom. Ginsburg brought in the peck of apples. With hardly so much as a look at him, Ida snatched an apple out of his basket and ran to her son's bedroom. It seemed to help him from the first bite; he demanded another apple. Ida ran back to get it. When she came into the parlor, the repulsive Ginsburg was staring ravished at Felice's photograph, which he had picked up from the floor.

From then on, Ida's conduct was not that of a rational being but that of a possessed one. "Mr. Ginsburg, are you a single or a married man?" she said with cold formality.

"I was married," said Ginsburg. "Your father, the Ramaz, knew my wife's family well. But my wife unfortunately died." This news also came to Ida as if by special delivery from Heaven—the second special delivery that morning.

Thereupon, another miracle occurred—one that always mystified Ida. As long as she had known Ginsburg, she had disliked his appearance without ever taking a really good look at him. Now she did take a god look at him and, marvellous to relate, he seemed to be tall, attractive, even handsome. "Tell me, Ginsburg," she said, still under a spell, "do you want to get married? I see you are looking at a high-born, educated girl who comes from my home town, Kroza. Do you want to get married, Ginsburg?" It was all a little too fast for Ginsburg; he stood there unable to speak, staring at the photograph in his hand, and his hand trembling. But Ida, borne along by a supernatural agency, extolled Felice's virtues as eloquently as if she had known her from babyhood, and she could see that

Ginsburg, like everyone else who looked at Felice's photograph, had melted. Ida's eloquence rose in a spiral of persuasion that would have moved a rock.

Ginsburg was no rock. Finally, he found speech. "A girl like this I would marry even at midnight, even in the dark," he said fervently.

Encouraged, lda became more realistic. "She has no money, Ginsburg. All she has is what you see in the picture."

"If she has half, I'll marry her," said Ginsburg gallantly.

"She's yours," said Ida lavishly, and then she added a cautionary postscript: "That is, if you get my husband's O.K."

Harry's O.K. proved not easy to get. When he was told of Levine's betrayal, he began breaking dishes. Then Ida told him of the Heaven-sent visitation of Ginsburg the peddler. Harry began to break more dishes. At the word "peddler," he grew apoplectic. His affection for Felice was so deep, his hopes for her so high, that he couldn't bear the idea of her allying herself with a worker in his own vineyard. "A peddler!" he shouted. "A wonderful girl like Felice should marry a peddler! Never till my dying day will I allow it! You call a peddler a wonderful catch?"

Even had the thought occurred to her, Ida would probably not have said that she didn't see why Felice should make a better match than she, the daughter of the Ramaz, had; Ida was too kindly for that. While Uncle Harry was picking up the last fragment of crockery, Ginsburg appeared. Instead of the nondescript costume he had worn the day before, he was now beautiful in a blue serge suit and a white shirt, not open at the throat like a poet's or a peddler's but with a tie, which gave him the appearance of a man of affairs. Moreover, he was now, Ida averred, at least two inches taller. He had become so good-looking that she felt she could have fallen in love with him herself. Nevertheless, she had to tell him that Harry would never permit Felice to marry a peddler. "But I am no peddler," said Ginsburg. "I have a store, but when things are slow there, I take to peddling to make a few extra dollars. Don't you worry about Felice. I will give her all the money she wants." Even Harry was impressed. When Felice arrived on Sunday to meet the capricious furrier from Atlanta, she met instead the only occasional peddler Ginsburg. The match was made.

When Ida was later asked whether she had received any fee for this marriage, she said, "I never took money from anybody. I did it for the pleasure. But from that time on, did my little *takhshidel* have apples!" ("*Takhshidel*" is a Yiddish expression meaning, loosely, "my darling one." It connotes intense affection, plus a tolerant awareness of imperfection; which of the two predominates depends entirely on the tone of voice.) The major emolument Ida derived from this happily consummated marriage was not her son's flood of apples but her joy at being able to write a withering letter to Levine, the tricky matchmaker from the Bronx. She often repeated the lofty sentences, simmering with quiet invective. She advised Levine thenceforward to keep his fake furriers to himself. As for Felice, he need not trouble his head in the least about her, since she could now announce Felice's engagement to the richest department-store owner in Worcester, a brilliant and cultivated millionaire who would, for all she knew, end up as Governor of Massachusetts.

After Ida moved to New York, she kept house for her father, whose second wife had recently died. Keeping house for the Ramaz was no light chore. Everybody came to his apartment—the rich, the poor, the halt, the lame, the blind. They came for help, for advice, for spiritual guidance, for relief in ritualistic dilemmas. About the last, the Ramaz was almost unique in tolerance, sympathy, and humor. To a woman who called him up to ask whether she could serve her family a chicken she had reason to believe had not been killed according to ritual, the Ramaz said, "I cannot possibly examine a chicken over the telephone." He tried to keep the woman from coming over by telling her to consult the rabbi in her own parish, but she made the journey to Eighty-fifth Street anyway. Ida received her, suspecting that the journey had been motivated by her desire to meet the wifeless Ramaz. Still, it was all grist to Ida's mill. The woman was a comely widow, and Ida married her off to a yearning elderly widower from Bradley Beach, in New Jersey. One day while her father was out, the doorbell rang and Ida opened the door to admit Jacob H. Schiff. Jacob Schiff was a reformed Jew; he normally attended the Temple Emanu-El. Obeying some atavistic impulse, however, when the time arrived for him to say his annual *Kaddish,* or memorial prayer, for his dead parents, he came to the Ramaz's synagogue to do it. Mr. Schiff asked for the Ramaz. Ida invited him to have a glass of tea while he waited for her father. Mr. Schiff accepted and, according to Ida, found her so agreeable that he said he would come one day and take her for a drive in the Park. Finally, he departed, leaving a message. When the Ramaz returned, Ida expatiated on Mr. Schiff's democratic manners. She was so dizzied by the vision of riding in the Park beside Jacob Schiff that she couldn't remember the message. When the Ramaz reproved her mildly, she said, "Don't worry. He'll be back any minute to take me for a ride." To which the Ramaz answered, with a tired smile, *"avahdah!"*—an untranslatable expression that conveys a maximum of affirmation firmly laced with a maximum of skepticism. The skepticism was, as it turned out, justified.

Ida immediately set about getting her father married again; it kept her hand in, and gave her a pleasant sense of piety. The Ramaz was then well over sixty, but there were many applicants for the position. He trusted Ida's discretion. There was one extremely persistent applicant who, in Ida's bitter words, haunted the funerals of the Ramaz's wives, "hoping, hoping, hoping." Ida settled on a less aggressive candidate, but it turned out that she had a bad heart, and within two years Ida had to do it all over again. On the day of her father's marriage to the woman with heart trouble, Ida left his house and moved to her youngest daughter's, on West Eighty-third Street. There—except for the twelve years she was married to a well-to-do Newark real-estate man named Newman—she spent the remainder of her life. The period before the marriage to Newman was a halcyon season of mad flirtation and feverish matchmaking. Many suitors came in quest of her; most of them she diverted to her clients. Her daughter's apartment was in perpetual turmoil.

The daughter, nicknamed Go-Go, had, as she still has, some of Ida's effervescence. This was Ida's explanation of why Go-Go, unlike her two sisters, had not remained in Worcester but had married a New Yorker. He was Maurice Bergman, a public-relations man and known to his friends as Bergie. Bergie adored Ida. Go-Go claimed that his devotion to Ida was so fervent because he spent long periods away from her in Hollywood. Actually, he didn't even mind the fact that Ida kept the line so busy talking to her prospects that he could never get his apartment on the telephone. Bergie's devotion to Ida wavered only once. Helmi, the Bergmans' Finnish cook, was an excellent cook and an institution in the family. But she was unmarried. There was also the elevator man, very shy and an expert on the weather. Bored with his meteorological predictions, Ida asked him one day whether he was married. He wasn't; he had thought about it, but no one was handy. "And what about Helmi?" said Ida. "She's a wonderful girl and a wonderful cook." Before the Bergmans knew what was happening, Helmi and the elevator man had got married and hired out in the country as a couple. Ida defended herself by saying that she couldn't stand the sight of lonely people.

"Helmi was not lonely!" said Go-Go, with some heat.

"The elevator man was lonely," said Ida.

Another character who impinged on the Bergmans' lives was known to them only as Box 77. After a morning of incessant phone ringing, Go-Go, who was waiting for a long-distance call from Bergie, finally answered the telephone herself. "It's for you," she said wearily to Ida. "It's a man and he won't give his name."

"If he doesn't give his name, I know who it is," said Ida.

The conversation went about as follows: "You didn't give your name, so you must be Box 77. I have a very nice party for you, Box 77—a very nice woman and she has a good business.... She lives in Bradley Beach.... You are a New Yorker and can't go to Bradley Beach.... Then what about a Philadelphia woman? Could you go to Philadelphia?... You are a printer and can't leave your business.... Well, thank you for calling, Box 77, and I'll see what I can do for you with a New York woman."

Another day, Go-Go was informed that Box 77 was in the lobby. Ida asked her to have him come right up. "Aren't you scared, Ma, to have a total stranger in the house?" Go-Go asked.

"A man who advertises in the Yiddish papers cannot be a stranger," said Ida primly. "You go into your bedroom; I will interview him in the living room."

From the bedroom, Go-Go listened while Ida interviewed Box 77: What was his ancestry? What about his printing business? Could he go out of town to interview prospects on Sunday? Would he give up his business for a Scranton woman who had a larger business? Finally, Box 77 departed.

"He sounded nice," said Go-Go. "How did you like him? Why didn't you speak for yourself?"

"He's a tall man and very nice," Ida said, "but he has a dot in one eye, and a man with a dot in the eye I couldn't marry. But I know lots of women who are not so particular." Ida did marry Box 77 off, and the Bergmans were enormously relieved.

In the field of matchmaking, Ida's major frustra-

tion was her only son, then an official of the
Federation of Jewish Philanthropies and now assistant director of the United Jewish Appeal, who also
lived in New York. He steadily resisted her strenu-
ous efforts to get him married. A friend, for reasons
known only to himself, nicknamed him the Major.
During the Second World War, the shortage of men
was acute and the clamor around Ida for husbands
became insistent and deafening. For a long time, her
son, who was then in his forties, was almost the
only good prospect on her list, but he was stubborn.
Once, she lined up for him an arithmetic teacher
with a dowry, but the teacher happened to have an
uncontrollable giggle. Ida admitted that she could
not understand how a girl so highly educated could
permit herself such a fatuous giggle. Then she mobilized a young woman who was a relative of
Professor Richard J. H. Gottheil, of Columbia. Ida's
sales talks usually featured important relatives, and
when she was selling her son, his relationship to the
Ramaz received due emphasis. Ida dilated on
Professor Gottheil's relative, and even improvised a
few glowing details about the professor's high
regard for the girl. Her son relented, then telephoned at the last moment to say that he could not
keep the appointment she had arranged for him. Ida
told him it would serve him right if the girl married
somebody else, and saw to it that she did. Another
problem was her discovery that the Ramaz's name
was not as potent among the younger set as it was

to her own generation. She had tantalized a mother who claimed to have an adorable young daughter by dangling before her the prospect of marrying this daughter off to the grandson of the Ramaz. To the astonishment of both mothers, the girl was not bowled over by the prospect; she had never heard of the Ramaz. She broke an appointment to meet the Ramaz's grandson in order to go to the Paramount and hear Frank Sinatra, leaving the Major to lunch with the two mothers. This was all right with him, for he was in the habit of coming up every Saturday to have lunch with his mother anyway, and found that reward sufficient, without the addition of romance.

Ida took to telephoning her son at his office for consultation and advice about her own romances. There was a violinist who played tender mazurkas to her over the telephone. Ida had called him back to tell him how thrilled she had been, and had got the violinist's daughter. The daughter, she reported, was cool. Ida sensed impending interference from her, and she was right; she received no more mazurkas on the telephone. Then there was a sportsman named Billikopf, a retired man who not only carried a cane but sported a "prince-nez" besides. One Saturday, Ida proudly showed her son a glass jar of salmon with her name on the label. Billikopf, she said, had caught the salmon, canned it, and labelled it with Ida's name and the date on which he had caught the fish. Things were going wonderfully when Billikopf, who had a way of travelling to far-off places, suddenly disappeared. Ida was sure that he had died—probably on a safari. It was years before she heard from him again. In the meantime, she used to say, with a sigh, "Ah, if only Billikopf had lived!"

Ida's son once wrote down a telephone conversation of his mother's: "Hello, *takhshidel*, I don't call you in the office too often. Why should I bother you? You are always busy. This time it's very important. I met a man who is interested in me and I would like you should look him up in John & Bradford what he has. Find out for me if he gives to Federation also. He told me he is a very charitable man. If he is rich like he says, he should give plenty. An educated man I know he is, but is he charitable? If he is not charitable, why should I bother with him? His business is with cedar chests and he told me that he and his son together do a very good business. But who knows? In John & Bradford you can find out for me. And besides, Sam, I heard of a wonderful girl for you in Bayonne. Her father is a heart specialist and her uncle . . . "

Ida's reputation became so far-flung that she received love letters from people she did not even know. This one is a fair example:

Dear Unknown Friend:

I came back to New York and thought of writing you. It's quite a long time I've been recommended to

144

write to you by Mr. Poles. We have corresponded for a while and then I had to leave town.

Should it happen that you're married at this time then I wish you luck. No harm of inquiring. In case you're still single and if you care I'd like to meet you some Saturday eve, or Sunday.

Yours sincerely,
Sam Miltz

As it happened, Ida *was* married at the time—to Newman of Newark, a marriage that she claimed she never could account for. Her detachment about this marriage may be gathered from the fact that after he died and she was asked why she did not wear mourning for him, she replied airily, "For my father, for my sister, for my mother, I will wear black. But why should I wear black for a total stranger?" Newman, who looked like Henri Poincaré, was a tall, corpulent, imposing man with a small, trim, pointed white beard. He was pious and adored the Ramaz, whom he had tried to entice to the rabbinate in Newark. As he could not have the Ramaz in Newark, he came to New York to see the holy man as often as possible, and summers, when the Ramaz was at Bradley Beach, he took his idol out for drives in his automobile, which the Ramaz enjoyed very much. Newman, who had done well in real estate, was now retired, and devoted himself to good works. He had two ambitions—to visit Palestine, and to visit it in the company of the Ramaz. Newman had settled in Newark by mistake. When he arrived in this country as an immigrant in his youth, he disembarked at Baltimore. It was his intention to go to New York, the only American city he knew. When the train reached Newark, however, he heard the conductor shouting what sounded to him like "New York," and he thought he had arrived at his destination. Several months passed before he found out he was not living in New York.

When Newman met Ida, who by then was fifty years old, at Bradley Beach, he fell in love with her at once. His double aspiration now became triple— to go to Palestine, to go with the Ramaz, and to go as the Ramaz's son-in-law. The ambition of Newman, who was close to sixty, paralleled that of Lord Rosebery, who set himself the goal of becoming, by thirty, Prime Minister of England, winner of the Derby, and husband of a Rothschild; it was equally intense and seemingly even less likely to be achieved. Newman, slow, ponderous, pontifical, became suddenly electrified when he beheld Ida's winsome blue eyes, and proposed to her. This was a reckless thing to do, considering (he did not tell this to Ida) that he had already been earmarked for a rich widow in Cleveland by Levine, Ida's old treacherous collaborator. Ida turned Newman down flat, but he persisted. He would take her and her father to Palestine on their honeymoon, he said. Ida said that she would like to go to Palestine, but not in a crowd. "You are in love with my father!" she exclaimed. "Why do you want me?" Privately she thought, as she later reported, "I should marry an old man with a white beard and a co-operation!" Newman made a strategic retreat. He would not press the matter now, he said, but he begged Ida to think it over. There was nothing for Ida to think over.

Ida, too, had a secret. She did not tell Newman that she was in love with a man named Blinkman, Go-Go's landlord, whose wife had just died. Ida had apparently been in love with him for a long time. Perhaps that was why she had not pinned down any one of her long succession of flirtations. But Blinkman was evasive. He had corresponded with Ida through three marriages, the first two arranged for him by Ida herself. Blinkman's letters, many of which have been preserved, show a variability in temperature. Those written while he was married are warm—just short of ardent—and full of complaints about his current wife, along with hints of the incumbent's shortcomings in comparison to Ida's perfections. Between marriages, the letters—many of them written in Miami Beach, expressing the wish that Ida were with him—are certainly courteous but somehow a little cool. Now Blinkman was free. Ida had only the other day sent him a special-delivery letter commenting on the coincidence that she was free, too; she had, as a matter of fact, been free for ten years. Newman's proposal, therefore, couldn't have come at a more unpropitious moment.

When ambition seizes certain temperaments, it is not to be gainsaid. Newman wrote Levine a letter ordering him to break off negotiations with the Cleveland widow and declaring that it was his intention to marry Ida, the daughter of the Ramaz. Levine was overcome. He had worked long and patiently to draw Newman and the widow together. As this was to be an alliance beyond the ordinary, because both people were rich, he had journeyed to Cleveland with Newman's photograph and credentials, and had journeyed to Newark with the widow's. Distracted, Levine wrote Newman a letter echoing an ineffectual Ibsen character before a comparable disaster: "People don't do such things!" Newman wrote back that he didn't care what people did. He knew what he was going to do; he was going to marry the daughter of the Ramaz. Levine replied that it was too late for Newman to change his course; the Cleveland widow had consented, and it was a pact. Newman wrote back that as he no longer consented, it was no pact. Levine, desperate, got on the subway and went to call on Ida.

Although Ida was not one to bear grudges, she had never entirely forgiven Levine for his conduct in the Fitchburg affair. True, the thing had turned out well; the Ginsburgs had been one of the most successful of her marriages. In business life, one has to make compromises, and Ida, over the years, had had various professional dealings with Levine. And now Levine stood before her a man bereft. What was this calamitous news, he wanted to know, about Newman of Newark? "Ask Newman!" said Ida crisply. Levine told her about what he called Newman's insane letters. He told her about the protracted negotiations with the Cleveland widow, a sensitive person of great breeding, to whom he had not dared even hint of Newman's perfidy. He intimated that if Ida would retire from the field, he would cut her in on the commission from the Cleveland-Newark alliance. This proffered bribe Ida rejected with disdain. There then took place one of those swift emotional reversals that dot the history of passion. Levine suddenly burst out with the information that he himself had always admired Ida—loved her, in fact. He was a lonely man, burdened with cares. He asked Ida to marry him. Ida was touched. Not until afterward did it occur to her that there might have been a mixture of motives, including a desire to remove a fleck from the carefully woven tapestry of the Cleveland-Newark marriage. Still, a proposal was a proposal.

"Levine," she said, "I cannot marry you, but thanks just the same."

Levine wanted to know why.

"I could not marry a marriage broker," said Ida.

Levine pointed out that it was a business in which she herself engaged, even though as an amateur.

"It's all right for a woman, but it's no business

for a man," said Ida.

Levine did not give up. They could pool their resources; he would go into some other business.

Ida decided to tell Levine the real reason. "My daughter's landlord's wife just died, so I want to marry him," she said.

Levine blinked. "You don't know?" he said incredulously.

"I don't know what?" asked Ida.

"Blinkman is going to marry Bernice from Queens," Levine said.

"Bernice from Queens I know very well. She is an old maid and deaf," Ida said.

"She won't be an old maid after Blinkman marries her," said Levine, "and she's only a little bit deaf."

Ida now knew why there had been no answer to her letter to Blinkman, but even in her disappointment, which she concealed from Levine, she wondered why, if Blinkman was going to marry Bernice, he hadn't asked her to arrange it. He had called her in on other occasions.

Now Levine returned to the attack. Would Ida marry him?

No, she couldn't possibly marry Levine. And she suddenly heard herself saying, "Levine, thank you for the compliment, but I can't marry you, because I am going to marry Newman of Newark. We are going with Papa to Palestine."

Later, trying to explain this astonishing statement, Ida speculated, in her detached way, on how she happened to make it. "How did I come to marry Newman of Newark?" she would ask. Then would come the various explanations. Perhaps it was pique over Blinkman. Perhaps—an ugly possibility she hoped was not true—she wanted to frustrate Levine's deal with the Cleveland woman out of revenge for Levine's behavior toward Felice. "Who knows?" Ida would say.

Presently, Ida did marry Newman of Newark, to her father's joy, and the three of them journeyed to Palestine.

In his long life, the Ramaz knew many griefs. In his boyhood and youth, in the famous rabbinical college at Telshe, in Lithuania, which was then part of Russia, he lived in deep communion with ancient sages, searching in the books and records they had left for the elusive essence of truth and goodness his faith told him must be somewhere behind all of life's sufferings. He sought identification with God. He was a mystic, but not in the Eastern sense; He did not believe that man's identification with the Eternal could ever be complete; human frailty being what it was, it could be only partial. The extent to which this identification could be enlarged was the measure of success in life, the only measure he knew. It was only because he was able to believe in the possibility of this development in every human

151

soul that life was not all pain and ashes. His erudition was vast, yet he never sank into the morass of pedantry, because he knew that even the sages he studied had not attained certainty but only the fleeting beauty of Divine intimation. This humility endowed the Ramaz with both mellowness and humor. He was amused at any kind of pretentiousness. During the time of Hitler, a group of prominent New Yorkers came to confer with the Ramaz about a program to help the German Jews. After the meeting was over, Ida went in to find the Ramaz looking sad. She asked him whether the meeting had gone well or badly. Her father pointed to the ashtrays brimming with cigar and cigarette stubs. "You can see from those that it was a successful conference," he said ruefully.

The Ramaz was still very young when people started referring to him as a *tzaddik,* or saint. He had recently emerged from the austerity and contemplation of the rabbinical college when, in 1886, he first received the call to go to the Baldwin Place Synagogue. He was then married to his first wife, a stately, pious, strong-minded young woman, whom he adored and who was with him through all his early tribulations. They had two sons and two daughters, their first child being Ida, who was ten when the Ramaz was summoned to Boston. Although he was received with great honor in Boston, he was bewildered and unhappy. The American scene was too alien; it was too bustling and ambitious and "progressive." He felt he could never make vivid and real to his parishioners the need he felt and, if he was to help them, the need they must feel. To the anger and dismay of the Bostonians, after a year in Boston he went back to his native town in Lithuania. On arriving there, he found a certain hostility in the atmosphere; the phrase "American rabbi" had in it the barb of epithet. It was as if he had vulgarized his gift, diluted his sainthood. This made him very sad, and he went back to the Baldwin Place Synagogue.

Shortly after the Ramaz returned to America, he and his wife sent their first son, who was then nine, back to Lithuania, to attend the Telshe rabbinical school. The Ramaz's ancestors had been rabbis as far back as the record could be traced, and he wanted his first son to be a rabbi; he feared that the boy would be caught up in the rush of American materialism and abandon the ancient faith. This fear was unfounded. The boy was precocious but devout. He received his *smicho,* or degree in Talmudic studies, when he was thirteen, a conspicuously early age for such an attainment, then came back to America and went to public schools and later to Harvard, where he made a brilliant record. Directly after his graduation, he was called to the rabbinate of the leading orthodox synagogue of Cleveland. In 1917, at the age of thirty-six, he was killed in an automobile accident. The Ramaz travelled to Cleveland to bring his son's body back to New York. He delivered the *hesped,* or eulogy, in his own synagogue. Those who heard it say that in the Ramaz's quiet voice and bearing they found comfort and reassurance. Many wept. The Ramaz did not weep. His son, he said, had had some identification with the Divine, the identification he himself had all his life striven to find. His son had found it, and perhaps, in his youth, and vigor, more clearly. He had, moreover, made the necessity for it clear to some of his parishioners, and thus his own vision was perpetuated. This made his brief life significant and imperishable.

In the family burial plot, the Ramaz had an extra grave. This was for his books—those that contained errors and those that were too worn to be rebound. The burying of blemished books was a common practice in Europe and is still done by some of the orthodox synagogues in America. To burn a book is considered a sin, just as it is considered a sin to burn the body. The Ramaz chose to bury his own books, as they became unusable, in the grave beside his own that he had provided for them. The marker on the Ramaz's other grave reads, in Hebrew, "Here lie the books and phylacteries that bore a blemish."

For the Ramaz, the advent of Hitler was the recurrence of an old pain. From his boyhood in Czarist Russia, he remembered persecution; he grew up in an atmosphere in which the constant threat of it was normal. He suffered now, but he did not share the panic of many of his parishioners, who feared that this virulence would cross the ocean. He gave them comfort, not so much by what he said as by his dignity and his calm faith that what the enemy believed in would perish and that what he believed in would survive. At the synagogue service on the eve of the Day of Atonement in 1934, after the singing of Kol Nidre, the Ramaz opened up the Ark and took out the Torah. "This," he said quietly, "is our faith, this is our strength, this is our hope." The Ramaz was eighty-two when, in the early days of the Hitler persecutions, he went to lead a mass meeting of twenty thousand people in prayer at Madison Square Garden. Even Ida was awed by the spectacle of the old man invoking Divine intercession to save the remnant of the Jewish people.

To the Ramaz, Ida was a peculiarly American phenomenon. He looked upon her with affectionate incredulity. She had been with him so much; they had weathered so many tragedies, both personal and racial, the Ramaz with his faith, Ida with her irrepressible gusto. He, who had endured so much sorrow, must have felt a certain exhilaration in the knowledge that his daughter was not wounded, that she enjoyed life as if it was not inevitably mottled with pain. To him, Ida was a creature from another world; he could not believe that he had produced her. Ida considered herself contemporary and down-to-earth. She thought her father dreamy and old-fashioned. To the Ramaz, Ida was like a character in an illuminated chapbook of the Middle Ages. In the spacious, distant chamber in which his thoughts dwelt, the reverberations of her activities reached him, yet he apprehended them but dimly. For him, they were like the hearsays bandied about by the medievalists—of strange wonders, of miracles, of monsters from undiscovered deeps, of unicorns, dragons, and demigods. He would inquire vaguely from time to time about her goings on; he was entertained by some of her exploits, as if, through an accident of research, he had come upon a gossip column from Cathay.

Anyone whose primary interest was not in romance was unrealistic to Ida, and Ida thought her father was unrealistic. Her romantic problems occasionally bordered on the ethical, and once, because Ida was at that time living with her father in New York, she brought him a nice one to adjudicate. It concerned the strange case of Anna Shapiro, a man whom Ida referred to as "the anxious Zionist," and an inventor. Anna was an old friend of Ida's, from her Boston days, and Ida had imported her from Boston to marry "a rich New Yorker." Everything was going wonderfully; the couple had two children and Anna was in seventh heaven. Then the husband developed a defect. "He got so rich that he went crazy," Ida said succinctly. Ida was sensitive about insanity among her clients. (Once, while she was living in Worcester, she had brought from Boston one of her best friends, a man named

Merrick, who was Commissioner of Weights and Measures, to marry a beautiful Worcester girl. Directly after the wedding ceremony, the bride began to yell and scream, and had to be taken to an institution for the insane. Merrick went back to Boston, and Ida followed him in order to explain that the bride's insanity was as much a surprise to her as it was to him. It took a conference of lawyers, rabbis, and judges to straighten the thing out. Merrick became cool toward Ida. "Nowadays," she said mournfully, "you have to be a doctor, a psy-what-do-you-call-it, as well as a matchmaker.") Anna put her husband in a sanatorium. One day, he threatened to kill himself unless the Ramaz came to see him, and Anna said that since Ida had brought her to this pass, the least she could do was get her father to go. The poor Ramaz went, and Anna's husband tried to enlist his interest in a project to build a subway from New York to Palestine. It was this proposal that caused Ida to dub him "the anxious Zionist." Unable to advance his project, the anxious Zionist did commit suicide. He left a substantial income to Anna, on the condition that she not marry again. This posed a problem. Anna was marriageable, but she didn't, as Ida said, "want to relax the money." One night, on the bench in the lobby of her father's apartment house, Ida fell to talking with an inventor. She had never met an inventor before, and as she had just lost Blinkman, she was in a receptive mood. When she went upstairs, she told her father she had met a scientist whom she could easily marry, but he needed money for his inventions. The Ramaz, without looking up from a book he was reading, said absently that impecunious inventors ought to be subsidized, and that Ida, in the interests of progress, might find him a rich wife. Ida wondered how a man could reach her father's age and understand so little about emotional involvement. She already saw herself the wife of a scientist, a position in life that seemed to her incredibly chic. But then, some days later, Ida found that the scientist was seeing Anna Shapiro. Anna had said nothing to her, her best friend, about it. Direct in everything, Ida approached Anna. Anna confessed that she loved the scientist. Would Ida further the match?

Ida came to the point at once. "Will you relax the money?" she asked.

"For him, yes," said Anna.

"Will you tell him that if he marries you, you will have to relax the money?" Ida asked.

At this, Anna's expression showed a certain tension.

"If I deal for you, I have to tell him," Ida said sternly. "He needs money for his inventions."

Anna temporized. "Let him invent without money," she said.

"If you don't tell him," Ida said, "I wash my hands!"

"Then wash," said Anna.

A coolness developed between the two old friends. Ida wrestled with the problem of whether to tell or not to tell. If she told, how would she know that she was not telling as a rival who wanted the scientist for herself, instead of as a disinterested marriage broker? It was her business to make marriages, and she had a moral obligation to Anna, because if it had not been for her, Anna would never have married the anxious Zionist. She found herself impaled on both horns of this dilemma. She decided to put the question to her father. After all, this was in a realm beyond romance; it involved ethics. She forced her father to stop reading and faced him with this new Judgment of Solomon. The Ramaz listened, took off his glasses, polished them, put them back. His clear blue eyes rested on his daughter. He remembered an odd anecdote of an ancestor to whom an analogous problem had been posed. It was a funny story, which had made rabbinical students laugh for four hundred years. Was this his daughter and was she living in the twentieth century? What a curious survival! Still, since Ida was so serious, he met the question with equal gravity. "If Anna wants you for an intermediary, you must persuade her to tell him," he said finally. "If she doesn't want you, then it's none of your business."

"Then I lose the match altogether," said Ida.

"You must persuade Anna to tell him," said the Ramaz. "Appeal to her vanity. Let her put the inventor to the test."

"And what about my conscience?" demanded Ida. " I like the inventor myself. What will Anna say if I marry him? She'll be mad, and she'll be right. What a business I chose, with such problems!"

"You won't have to worry about your conscience," said the Ramaz. "If the inventor won't marry Anna without money, then he won't marry you. The probability is he will return to his science. By the way, *töchterel*, what did your scientist invent?"

"He has just made an invention the salt and the pepper should come from the same shaker," Ida said.

The Ramaz looked profoundly impressed. He predicted the eclipse of Einstein and returned to his books.

Ida persuaded Anna to inform the scientist of her difficult financial status, and for a season the scientist did, indeed, disappear into his laboratory. Eventually, Anna and Ida patched things up, on the common ground that scientists were scum. But later, when Ida got a letter from the inventor, she admitted that her heart missed a beat. It was a strange letter for a scientist to write, since it took the form of a poem. It was more than a poem; it was a poetic anagram. It was written on the stationery of the scientist's firm—the All-In Mfg. Co.—and bore a picture of a salt-and-pepper shaker. The first letters of the poem's eleven lines spelled out the greeting "Good morning." After the first thrill, Ida felt let down.

"Good morning is not love," she said. "He could just as well send me good night!"

When Ida married Newman and went to Newark to live, her father was happy. But Ida did not fully share the Ramaz's feeling that all was well. Newman was proud of her, and Ida was a good wife to him. The difficulty was that she didn't care for Newark. To her, it was almost like living in Worcester. True, she never saw a bear there, but it was benchless and provincial. She confessed that she enjoyed going to Worcester just to get away from Newark. She regretted her husband's mistake in getting off the train in Newark when by staying on a half hour longer he could have got off in New York. "What a difference in that half hour!" she summarized elegiacally. She kept up her New York connections, and she was always in and out of town. Summers she spent at Bradley Beach, driving about with her husband and her father. Bradley Beach was teeming with the unmarried—young people, widows, widowers. She accumulated enough prospects there to keep her busy through the winters. As Mrs. Ida Newman, she felt that she had emerged from bohemia and was firmly established in the upper bourgeoisie. She had acquired status apart from her father. On a visit to Worcester, she asked one of her daughters if she would take a check. Her daughter asked if she needed cash. "No, no," said Ida, "I don't need cash. I just thought you would like one of my checks for a souvenir." She produced one; it had printed on it, "Mrs. Ida Newman, 222 West 83 Street, New York, N.Y." Ida enjoyed handing around her checks like calling cards. She used a New York address—actually, Go-Go's address—because she insisted on maintaining her metropolitan standing; she saw no reason to recognize Newark as her place of residence simply because, on account of her husband, she happened to live there.

In 1938, Newman died, and Ida moved back to Go-Go's. Box 77 was on the phone again. Before long, Go-Go was busy heading an organization that supplied theatre tickets to service men, and she was forced to make a rule that there were to be no calls from Ida's prospects until after one in the afternoon. Ida sent out a bulletin to all her clients. She did her best to make them obey the rule, but it cramped her style. Once, her son-in-law, shaving in the bathroom, heard her say on the telephone, "Hello....You have the wrong number, but call me up after one o'clock."

He came out of the bathroom to inquire, "If it's the wrong number, why did you ask whoever it was to call after one?"

"Because," she said, "I can take my calls after one, and who knows? He had such a nice voice. Sounded like an educated man!"

When the Ramaz's third wife died, Ida took the

death as a reflection on her own ability. She determined that the next one must have a doctor's certificate. She did not really want to leave Go-Go's to keep house for her father—she would have to send out so many cards to announce the new telephone number. She acted with dispatch; in fact, she married her father off without leaving Go-Go's apartment. She referred to this coup as "the window marriage." Ida was sitting by a window reading when a window in the opposite apartment opened and a nice-looking gray-haired woman addressed her across the narrow areaway. "Dearie, I heard that your father's wife died," she said. "I would like an introduction."

"Are you pious?" Ida asked.

"I am pious, but for your father I could be more pious."

"Are you healthy?" Ida asked.

"I never had a sick day."

"I had in mind a Boston woman," Ida said.

"Why should he go to Boston when I am right here?"

"I will let you know," Ida said.

She informed her father that there was a beautiful woman next door who had always greatly admired him and who asked nothing more of life than to be his wife. She then had a doctor examine the woman, and he reported that her heart was good. The marriage took place.

Before long, this woman, too, became ill. Ida

called in the doctor. "I thought you said her heart was good," she said.

"Her heart is good," said the doctor, "but her lungs are not so good."

"After my mother," Ida used to say sadly, "Papa never had any luck with his wives." Actually, however, the Ramaz's fourth wife survived him.

Ida was in the full tide of her activities when, at the age of sixty-nine, she was stricken with her last—and, indeed, her first—illness. For a year, she was in and out of hospitals. To arrest the course of her disease, her doctors decided to amputate her right foot. Henceforth, Ida spoke of "the foot" as if it were someone who had turned on her although she had never offered it anything but kindness. She began to blame everything on "the foot." Had it not been for "the foot," she could have married this one or that one. In the hospital, everybody—the doctors, the nurses, her surgeon, even the invisible patient in the room next door—loved Ida. She discovered that her surgeon lived with his mother. Between his work and his mother, he told her, he hadn't time to look for girls. Ida understood this. She could see how devoted he was to his patients; naturally he had no time to look for girls. It was for men of his sort that she existed. "When we get you out of here and well, we'll talk about it," he told Ida. She said she felt very well; "the foot" was only a minor inconvenience. If there was anything in the world that was in acute demand among the mothers of unmarried girls, she said, it was a doctor—especially a surgeon. The surgeon hedged; he couldn't leave his mother. ("He has a silver-corded mother," Ida told her son.) She informed the surgeon that mothers were all very well—she was one herself—but that they shouldn't interfere with their sons' happiness. To the end, Ida dangled prospects before the surgeon. He told Go-Go that talking to Ida about his matrimonial prospects gave him all the fun without any of the responsibility.

In the hospital, Ida had an Irish nurse who was so pretty that Ida said she could eat her up. Ida lamented that she had no Irish connections; if only she had some, she told the nurse, she could make a match for her in a minute right from bed. The patient next door sent Ida a rose, with a note saying that his nurse's stories about her had cheered him up. In another note, he said that if he got well he would like to marry Ida. Ida did not take this literally, but she wrote back telling him to get well anyway. The roses kept coming. One day, Ida's nurse told her that the man wanted to be wheeled in for a visit. "He thinks I am beautiful," Ida said. "If he comes in, he will see I am an old woman. He will be disappointed. Better he should keep sending me roses!"

In her tussle with "the foot," Ida's vanity suffered. "If it has to come off, perhaps we should move into a new neighborhood," she said to Go-Go before the operation. Ida had to have a special shoe made, but she implored her doctor to have it made with a high heel. When she left the hospital, she limped slightly, and she took this as punishment from God, because she remembered that when she was a little girl in Kroza she had imitated a woman who limped. The operation only delayed the end. After six months of limping about on her high-heeled shoes, Ida was forced to take to her bed. She knew she was going to die, and she faced it with equanimity, even with gaiety. "When I die, there will be joy in Heaven among the unmarried angels," she predicted. She was a long time dying; her deathbed was a prolonged social causerie—like Heine's, plus, of course, her matchmaking. Conscious that time was running out, she increased the pressure on her son. She gave him a diamond ring that had belonged to her mother, asking him to give it to his bride if he ever got one. She suggested to him that he call up the arithmetic teacher, in the hope that the years had moderated her giggle. (As it turned out, he got married two years later, to a girl that he found without his mother's help.)

Everybody came to see Ida, sometimes to exchange jokes, sometimes to commiserate. Many of her visitors she didn't know at all. Most trying were the visits of the ladies of the synagogue, who sat around with mournful expressions—expressions they should have reserved for her funeral, she said.

A couple of them shook their heads and murmured, "Our dear Mrs. Newman isn't ours any more."

"When was I theirs?" Ida demanded, within their hearing.

She enjoyed shocking the ladies of the synagogue. She would improvise the *hesped* that would be said over her: "The daughter of the great Ramaz has gone from us. He prepared people to live in Heaven, the daughter prepared them to be happy on earth." The ladies shuddered at the blasphemy and departed.

One day, Ida asked to have her doctor visit her. "I have a new lover," she told him. Her doctor, prepared for anything, asked her who he was. "Pain is my new lover," she said. Another day, to her astonishment, Billikopf, the salmon fisherman, came to see her. For years, Ida had thought he was dead; his arrival made her feel that she had already reached the farther shore. It was, she said, "like one ghost entertaining another ghost." Couriers from the benches brought her bulletins; while she lay ill, two men she had met on the benches—one of them an extraordinary catch, for he smoked expensive cigars—had died. She mourned these deaths, which she called premature, by which she meant that the benchers had died before she was able to settle them. "If I weren't so sicky-weaky, what I could have done!" she said.

When an oxygen tent was brought in, she said calmly, "That is what Papa had when he died. Now

I have the entrée to die. The Malach Hamoves has invited me. It is like when you get an invitation from the president of the synagogue to a party with on the bottom engraved R.P.V.S. You don't want to go, but it's the president of the synagogue—you have to go." She sent for her son and gave him a slip of paper on which she had written a date—her birthday and a year—with a blank line for the date of her death. She asked the Major to put this birth date on her tombstone. He noticed that she had lopped off fifteen years, but he said nothing. Ida looked at him, her blue eyes twinkling. "I know what you are thinking, *takhshidel*," she said, "but just think! Before my tombstone, people will be coming and going. Maybe if you put on this date, they will stop and look. Who is interested in an old woman? This way, they will stop. 'Ah,' they will say, 'the daughter of the Ramaz! Poor girl! What a pity she died so young!'"

7

THE IMPROVEMENT IN
MR. GAYNOR'S TECHNIQUE

One morning I awoke with a passionate urge to learn to play the piano. I must have been about twelve or thirteen years old. Later that day, I communicated the news of this burning desire to Willie Lavin. Willie, it seemed to me then, could accomplish anything; perhaps he could make me a pianist. In any case, he was the only person in the world to whom I could confide so bizarre an ambition without being thought completely insane. We had, of course, no piano in our tenement, and I certainly had no money for lessons even if we had had one. I might as well have wished to go abroad to study, or to get a motorcycle, or to fly to the moon. The impulse was grotesque, it was aberrational—but it was also imperious. I could not wait.

My friendship with Willie was in itself as bizarre as my wish to learn about music. The gap of six or seven years between our ages was millennial and it was, by ordinary standards, unbridgeable. Willie was a visitor from another planet, whose orbit for a long time did not coincide with my own. I remember lying in my bed at night when I was seven or eight years old and hearing him and my brother and their friends exchange the day's gossip in the living room. Assuming that I was asleep, they were uninhibited in their confidences, and I used to wonder drowsily how fellows as intelligent and mature as Willie and his friends could spend so much of their time talking about girls. Certainly the subject preempted a large part of their conversation.

There was a period when the craze for dancing swept over these elderly adolescents like a mania. A waltz was then fashionable in which, at a crucial point, you dipped your knee against your partner's in a kind of violent curtsy. The timing and audacity of this dip, and its possible emoluments in a larger gambit, the exact scope of which I could not fathom, were discussed thoroughly, in a way that was at once tantalizing and irritating. One of the liveliest of my brother's friends, Dan Eisner, who had the inside track with Myra Ellender, was a particularly accomplished amorist. He bought large white silk handkerchiefs and would place one between his hand and Myra's back while he was dancing with her. Myra appreciated this refinement, he said.

To these mesmerized youths the only thing that mattered at the moment was the reaction of girls in canoes and on the dance floor. There were debates on conflicting theories. Some said it was more climactic to go canoeing first and *then* go to the dance hall; the reverse procedure had equally sincere advocates. It all was a nuisance to me, lying there in the dark and listening. Once, after recounting an exploit with perhaps too much vividness, one narrator became suddenly conscious that I was in the next room. I heard him say to my brother, "Is the kid asleep?" My brother looked in on me. I remember watching, through half-shut eyes, his precautionary glance through the door. Reassured by my brother, the cad went on to narrate his triumph.

To me, my brother and all his friends seemed old, and I used to reflect that the attainment of so great an age must be in some way a degenerative process. I recall, for example, that at one period the group seemed to have gone suddenly demented on the subject of barbers. My mother used to cut my hair when it needed it, and I had never been in a barbershop. But these gentlemen had begun to shave, and before special occasions they used to go to the barbershop in the Hotel Warren for shaves and haircuts. There was even lordly talk of massages, and the merits of each barber were discussed

ad nauseam. I remember an argument about one barber, named Toussaint, whose obstinacy was so styl-
ized that he insisted on cutting Willie's hair not
according to Willie's ideas but according to his own.
One day, Willie had rebelled and switched to another chair. His revolt was discussed passionately, in
terms of a major insurrection. Toussaint had ardent
defenders, and tempers rose. There was a lot of talk,
too, about lotions and pomades. The effects of a too
pomaded head on a canoe pillow, and even on a
sofa pillow, when in the company of a girl came in
for nice adjudication. It was all very disillusioning.
I didn't mind about my brother and the rest—they
could be as inane or vacuous as they liked—but that
Willie should participate so fanatically in the heated
evaluation of these trivia caused me pain. Finally I
had a revelation that set my disturbed mental life in
order: When Willie was with me, talking about
books or ideas or poetry or going to college, he was
his true self; his discussions with his own crowd
were merely the diplomatic adjustments necessary
to a man of the world involuntarily caught up in a
corrupt and busy social whirl. Everything was all
right as far as Willie and I were concerned after that.

It is still something of a miracle to me that, when
I told Willie about my wish to play the piano, he
took it in his stride, as if it were the most natural
thing in the world. He had an odd habit of grasping
at a subject in its most generalized terms, never in
its immediate, specific application, and he also had

a habit of reading up exhaustively on each of his interests in turn. This idiosyncrasy of Willie's was recognized by his friends and he was often teased about it. One day, my brother, who had just discovered that some people went fishing, suggested that Willie try fishing in Lake Quinsigamond. Willie seized upon the idea at once with great enthusiasm and held forth on the importance of hobbies as a relaxation for busy men. My brother told me long afterward that Willie never actually went fishing— he'd got too tangled up in the *theory* of the sport to have time to practice it. He had gone at once to the Worcester Public Library and got out a quantity of books on rods, lines, fly-casting, bait-fishing, salmon and trout fishing—although there were neither trout not salmon in Lake Quisigamond—and devoured them all. So when I made known my ambition to master the piano, Willie became instantly dithyrambic. Within a half hour, we were in the Library, on Elm Street, and presently emerged with two books by James Huneker—the one on Chopin, and *Melomaniacs*. (Spurred on by Willie, I eventually read everything by Huneker the Worcester Library had, so that by the time I got to New York some years later I knew all about him. My first visit to Luchow's Restaurant was inspired by the fact that I had read somewhere that Huneker went there. I asked the head waiter if my hero was around, allowing him to believe that I was an important figure in Huneker's world, and when I was told that he was not, I went out on Fourteenth Street to Walton's for lunch. I have often wondered what would have happened if Huneker *had* been there.)

In his enthusiasm, Willie imagined me already a virtuoso, walking into a drawing room and captivating the distinguished guests by my art. To play the piano beautifully would be not only a social passport, he said, but also a relaxation for me after the vortex of a fevered day. (Willie was always preparing for a future in which we would both be under mighty strains.) He insisted that a powerful argument could be made for music as the greatest of arts, and quoted many people who thought so. It was even possible to conjecture that Beethoven was greater than Shakespeare, for whom, Willie knew, I already had a high regard. Did I not know huge portions of *Hamlet* and *Macbeth* by heart, and had he not incited me to repeat them to my brother when the latter asked what the hell Willie was doing hanging around with an embryo like me? Willie was happy that I had had this wonderful idea of learning to play the piano; he rather reproached himself for not having had it for me himself. He did not wish me to decide on the instant whether Beethoven was greater than Shakespeare, he said, but what he did wish was to make it possible for me, after having plumbed both these artists, to decide the question for myself. Pending my ultimate decision, Willie asked for time to give the matter a little thought himself. I permitted him to have it.

Willie's fantasia left me excited but unsatisfied during our preliminary discussions, but I believed in the omnipotence he had demonstrated on many occasions where my affairs were concerned, and soon he came to me with a *fait accompli*. He had engaged for me the use of a room with a piano in it, on Pleasant Street, and I could go there to practice for several hours every afternoon. He had telephoned to Mr. Silas Gaynor, one of the best music teachers in Worcester, and had made arrangements for me to study with him. He took me to the room and showed me the piano, and then escorted me to Mr. Gaynor's studio and introduced me to him. Mr. Gaynor gave me pleasant encouragement, some exercise books, and an appointment at his studio for the following week. On our way home to Providence Street, Willie, rather flushed with pleasure at having, singlehanded, transformed a novice into a virtuoso, congratulated me on having become a musician. I was somewhat appalled and asked Willie about the financial implications of these proceedings. He deprecated the intrusion of the money question into the exalted realm of the fine arts. What were the few pennies involved compared to the mystery of so great an art? I was not to think about the cost; he would take care of that. I was to become a nimble executioner, and he would be amply rewarded by the pride he would feel at my first recital. He brushed away the economic aspect with so high a hand that I withdrew the vulgarism. Willie imposed but one condition on me; no one was to know about my secret studies, least of all my brothers. I solemnly promised.

My career began. I had a permanent patron, which is more than Mozart ever had. I was a freshman in the Classical High School by this time, and it was on the same side of town as my piano. Instead of going straight home every afternoon, as had been my custom, I would tell my mother some lie about having to stay after school and go directly from Classical High to Pleasant Street. It was odd to sit down at a piano in a strange room—the instrument itself, by its very presence, connoted a degree of opulence that was faintly illicit—and to begin fumbling over Mr. Gaynor's scales. I had never before had command of a room away from my parents' flat. But it was easier to command the room than the upright. Also, I was conscious, while I was practicing, that this must be costing Willie a lot of money, and although I attacked the exercises fiercely, every time I muffed a bar, I seemed to hear the ominous tolling of invisible cash registers. I soon saw, too, that my entrance into elegant salons aquiver to hear me perform must be indefinitely delayed. Beethoven seemed farther away now than he had in my first excited talks with Willie. Possibly I was drawing nearer to the Master—at least, so Willie assured me when I confided to him my discouragements—but the speed of my approach was too slow and my progress too halting to give me any reassurance.

There were other difficulties. To keep my secret pact with Willie and the piano involved considerable ingenuity. My brother, after a complaint from my mother, began to ask why I was so late getting home from school every day. There were chores that I was relied on to perform after school, and the conflict between my domestic life and my career began to interrupt the normal flow of existence. My lies multiplied and finally wore so thin that I felt certain I would be exposed in the end. But for a month or so Willie's new plan for me seemed pleasingly dangerous, conspiratorial, and altogether wonderful. The only thing really dreary about it was the drudgery of practicing, which, as countless other young people have discovered, is a process that carries in it the germ of hatred for the art it is meant to further.

I adored Mr. Gaynor, and I shall never forget my first lesson with him, nor, indeed, the eight or ten subsequent ones. He was (and still is, I hope) a fair-complexioned man with light hair parted in the middle, and faintly protuberant, mild blue eyes that peered benevolently at you from behind thick glasses. He had a passion for music. At the first lesson, after I had ravished him with the results of my week's labors, he talked to me about music. His enthusiasm was as keen as Willie's, but it had greater intimacy. As I found it more delicious to discuss music than to play it, I spurred him on. He told me that every week he went to Boston to hear the concerts in Symphony Hall, which were then under the direction of Dr. Karl Muck. He described the program he had heard the week before and regaled me with anecdotes about the steely Dr. Muck and his Brahmin audiences. He had a strong sense of humor, and he was gently derisive of the pseudo-music lovers who went to Symphony Hall only because it was the correct thing to do in Boston on Friday afternoons or Saturday evenings. But I really wanted to find out about music, and somehow—I don't know how I had the courage —I found myself asking Mr. Gaynor if he would play something for me. I had never been to a concert. I had never heard a professional pianist. The nearest I had come to it was to stand outside Mechanics' Hall on an evening when Paderewski was playing inside and watch the crowd go in. Sensually, there was something insubstantial about this experience, and perhaps it was the frustration engendered by it that gave me the courage to ask Mr. Gaynor to play for me. Somewhat to my surprise, Mr. Gaynor responded readily. Perhaps I was the first pupil who had ever made such a request of him. He blushed faintly, but he went at once to the piano (his was a grand), sat before it, and played Schumann's "Aufschwung." I shall never forget it. It was thrilling. It was thrilling, but at the same time it made me rather miserable, because I could not help comparing my own performance with his.

My first séance with Mr. Gaynor was a model of our later ones, except that as I became more and more conscious of the immense discrepancy between our respective talents, I began to reduce to a minimum my performances to him and to induce him gradually to increase his performances to me. Also, we used to escape from such dull minutiae as scales and exercises by discussing the larger aspects of music. As I look back on it, it was not a bad use of our time, since it was unlikely that my secret life in art could continue for long. And I like to think that Mr. Gaynor, too, enjoyed our lessons. They gave him a chance to talk freely about the art he loved, and also to play for me many works that he must have been too tired to run through at night, after his long day at his studio. He was a very popular teacher—"the best in Worcester," it was often said—and I got the same odd thrill of creative patronage from hearing him that Willie must have got from hearing me. On the first day, when he played the "Aufschwung," Mr. Gaynor seemed to me to play it wonderfully. As he got into his swing during subsequent lessons, he began to play longer and more complicated works, and I felt—was it really so or was it merely the wish fulfillment of an eager patron?—that his technique was improving sensibly. By the time I left him, I think I may say that he was playing in really masterful style. I had every reason to be proud.

Leave Mr. Gaynor I did. Things began to happen thick and fast. The incessant questionings at home about my late-afternoon disappearances had given way to an ominous silence. Then, one afternoon, when I was blindly practicing on Pleasant Street, there was a knock on the door. I rushed to open it, sure that it must be Willie, who often used to drop into my atelier to tell me, when I was depressed about my work, that Brahms had never been a very good pianist, either. Gradually, Willie had modified his ambition for me; he had adjusted himself to the compromise that I need not become a dazzling virtuoso, and had settled for my evolving merely into a great composer, a career that while I was stumbling over Mr. Gaynor's exercise books seemed much the easier of the two. But the knock on the door was not Willie. It was my brother. He had followed me to my lair. When Mr. Gaynor told me, at my next lesson, that the opening bars of Beethoven's Fifth symbolized the knocking of Fate, it was my brother's knock on the door of my secret music room that I heard, and even now, when I hear those measures played, I hear that knock again.

I told my brother all, and he was much nicer about it than I could have hoped. He simply explained to me that music might be all right enough for those who could afford it, but that as I could not, I should not indulge myself with thoughts above my station. He caused me considerable pain by pointing out to me that although Willie

was better off than we were—as, indeed, who was
not?—he still had to work Saturdays and Sundays
and holidays and evenings in order to put himself
through Worcester Tech, and that to launch me on a
musical career involved considerable extra expense
for him. I was overcome suddenly by the enormity
of my own selfishness. Later, I discovered that my
lessons had cost Willie three dollars a week—two
dollars for the room and the piano, and one dollar
for Mr. Gaynor. Three dollars a week was no mean
sum in Worcester then, and to enjoy the luxury of
patronage Willie must have had to make many sac-
rifices. I also found out later that my brother and
Willie had a big fight about this. Willie contended
stoutly that three dollars a week was nothing at all
compared to the magnificence of the vista opened
up by my entry into the music world. Willie lost out.
I gave up Pleasant Street.

There followed an odd postlude. I gave up my
room and my piano, but I could not bear to give up
Mr. Gaynor. I had grown very fond of him. Possibly
I felt, obscurely, that a few more weeks with me
would give his playing that reserve and polish that
so often differentiate the routine pianist from the
really exceptional one. Willie encouraged me to continue my sessions with Mr. Gaynor—for a while, at
any rate. After all, it was only a dollar a week, and I
could manage this one hour without complications
at home. I used to report to Willie in detail on my
meetings with Mr. Gaynor, and from these reports

Willie derived a glow of satisfaction. On one occasion, he telephoned to Mr. Gaynor to find out how I was getting on, and Mr. Gaynor reported that I was extremely musical. There was the problem, of course, since I was no longer able to practice at all, of how to get by the mortifying introductory interval when I played for Mr. Gaynor and into the halcyon one in which he played for me. I managed this for a while by simply repeating exercises that I had already learned and, thus, for a brief spell, I was in the rather gratifying position of the eighteenth-century German princes who had their own virtuosos to console them. I think I may say with confidence that I was the only resident of Providence Street at that time who had a private pianist.

The day came when Mr. Gaynor gave me a fresh exercise book, and then I had to break down and tell him I had no piano. He had never known that I practiced on a rented piano in a rented room; he had, naturally, assumed that, like his other pupils, I had an instrument at home. I did not give my secret away. Instead, I invented the lie that my family had sold our piano, because we were moving out of town. I think there was genuine regret on Mr. Gaynor's part when we said good-bye. I promised that should there be a change in the family plans, in which case we would, of course, repurchase our piano, I would resume his auditions at once. I don't know whether Mr. Gaynor, in the long roster of his pupils, remembers me, but I remember him with affection and with joy.

This, then, was my brief encounter with that tantalizing art in which, more than in any other, I should have loved to become accomplished. But it was not to be. The little I learned on Pleasant Street I have long since forgotten. To this day, music remains a black art to me. I sit before it, but I have no actual notion of it. I do not understand it at all. I cannot read the language in which it is written; I am, and always shall be, an outsider.

8

MY ROMANCE WITH
ELEONORA SEARS

S ome years ago when I was in Boston for a brief
stay, a friend called me at my hotel and asked
me if I would go with her that afternoon to
have tea with Miss Eleonora Sears. I demurred. My
friend misunderstood my hesitation and began to
bolster her invitation with a host of facts about Miss
Sears: she was the most spectacular daughter of a
long line of Boston Searses, famous in her youth for
feats of strength and skill and endurance; a débu-
tante of the early nineteen-hundreds who had kept
on going for years after she came out; one of the first
well-known American girl athletes and, in a way,

the first of the outdoor girls; ex-tennis champion, equestrienne, athlete at large, friend of man and beast—Boston at its briskest, Boston at its most emancipated. As my hesitation nevertheless continued, the encomiums came faster and finally gathered into an avalanche of satiric invective. It was high time for me to abandon this pose of shyness. Miss Sears was friendly and simple and nobody to be afraid of, and, in any case, my friend would be right over to fetch me.

Had she but known it, she did not have to tell me about Miss Sears. My hesitation had been due to amazement; I was stunned by this sudden and unexpected intrusion of the actual into the legendary. For I had suffered over Miss Eleonora. Because of my youthful preoccupation with her, I had endured the taunts of my companions when I was a boy. For many years, I was not only in love with Miss Sears but, as I shall later explain, I had made with her an identification of which she was unaware. Thus when my friend tossed this astonishing invitation into my lap, it was as startling to me as if I had been an art-struck youth asked casually to go to a tea dance with Venus de Milo or to drop in for lunch with Mona Lisa. I knew, of course, that Miss Sears still existed and that she was in all probability almost as active a lady as she had been when, in my adolescence, I had cut her pictures out of the Boston papers. I had known then that she existed, but I had not thought that it was in a world where one could go and see her. She might just as well have been living on Mars.

Actually, I owed Miss Sears for more than serving as the unwitting object of my affections. Through her, I got my first glimpse into the mysterious and rather frightening world that I sensed must be spinning outside the close confines of Providence Street. The revelation came one summer morning when I was making my daily trudge to Lake Quinsigamond. It was an illumination, not, perhaps, as profound or disturbing or epochal as those described in the memoirs of the saints and prophets, but cozier.

Miss Sears first attracted me by wearing a derby hat. I had thought that this was a form of headgear reserved especially for men; my uncles, who were peddlers and small tradesmen, wore derbies. When I came upon a news picture of Miss Sears in hers, I saw at once that she did it with more chic. The photograph—from the Sunday magazine section of the Boston *Herald*, I believe—also showed her getting on a horse. There was something about her that appealed to me so strongly that I cut the picture out and tucked it into the frame of the mirror over the bureau in my bedroom. This was a mistake. One of my best friends saw the picture when he dropped in the next morning to pick me up for our walk to Lake Quinsigamond. He was contemptuous; in *his* bedroom, he pointed out disdainfully, he had William McKinley.

Lake Quinsigamond was a lovely lake—or so it seemed to us then—four miles long, dotted with islands, about four miles distant from the triple-decker tenement houses of Providence Street. In summer we boys went to sleep at night dreaming of the Lake and of the moment when we would arrive the next morning at what we called "the tank"—a swimming pool built at the edge of the water and presided over by a wizened deity in trunks named Jerry Daly. Non-swimmers and weak swimmers were confined to the tank. The great day was when Jerry considered you an able enough swimmer to be allowed to dive from the platform outside and swim in the Lake itself. And the feat for which, as we grew older, we lived and labored was to swim from Jerry Daly's to an island about a mile and a half distant. The day I accomplished this, I felt an ecstasy of achievement I have not known since.

There was a trolley to the Lake, but for us boys from Providence Street the five-cent fare was prohibitive. Every day of our summer vacation, we would roll our bathing trunks into towels and walk to the Lake for a blissful hour or two with Jerry Daly, and then walk home again. There was a tradition among us that swimming in the rain had a special excitement, so storms did not deter us. We would walk down the steep decline of Providence Street, past the dingy small shops of Grafton Street, with their proprietors lounging skeptically in the

doorways, waiting for customers, until we came to
the old Union Station, with its tall clock tower,
where we were sometimes held up for twenty minutes by the slow crawl of interminable freight
trains. This station was very familiar to me, principally because, to satisfy an itch for travel, I had
often boarded the incoming trains from Springfield
or Boston and sat on the plush seats while the train
stopped to take on Worcester passengers. I would
get off at the last minute before departure, with the
worldly air of one who has just completed a fatiguing journey. Beyond the station began the upgrade
of Shrewsbury Street, which was almost as steep as
Providence. It climbed into Belmont Street, and
Belmont led to the Lake. We would settle down to
the long climb like passengers settling down for a
transcontinental tour, and pass the time by discussing technical questions about the breast stroke
and the Australian crawl. On lower Shrewsbury
lived the Italian colony, and the women were usually out on summer days, hanging up their washing. On the Fourth of July, the fireworks display
furnished by this group of citizens was the most
flamboyant in town. Almost at the end of the long
trek, we would pass the State Insane Asylum. That
was always a landmark we were glad to see ahead,
for when we got to it, we knew the promised water
was tantalizingly near. We would cross the street to
get closer to the fence around the great enclosure of
the Asylum, because in that way we could some-

times catch glimpses of the inmates, who would glower and scream at us or laugh obscenely, and this was both terrifying and diverting. Many years later, when I was at Harvard and taking a course in abnormal psychology, my class made a trip to inspect this very institution. I remember a horrid demonstration of a disease of immobility; a patient's arm, pushed up into the air by an attendant, remained fixed where the attendant put it and the sufferer's position would not change, although it was grotesquely uncomfortable, until the attendant moved the arm down again. I remember, too, that I looked away from this spectacle for a moment and realized suddenly that from here I could easily get to Jerry Daly's. But it was December, and we were summoned peremptorily to inspect some paretics.

The Lake took you right through the various stages of adolescence; it was the focus of a mass libido. At first, your god was Jerry Daly. When you got a little older, it was Mr. Coburn, the proprietor of Coburn's Boat House, at whose establishment, for twenty-five cents an hour, you might rent a rowboat or a canoe. When we young stalwarts took to rowing, four or five of us would chip in to hire a boat for an hour. Canoeing was considered effeminate, and we made fun of the older boys who took girls out in canoes. But a day came when we did it ourselves, and from then on the reign of Jerry Daly receded. Graceful manipulation of the canoe became the ideal, rather than feats of endurance and strength in the water. One summer, there was a revolution, when we all abandoned ordinary paddling and took up the "Indian stroke." This meant that you never took your paddle out of the water but instead right-angled it swiftly at the end of each stroke and cut the water, as if with a blade, for the next push. Once we had mastered the stroke, we felt swanlike.

The Providence Street mothers had a special hatred for canoeing. Canoes were volatile and dangerous. Jerry Daly used to boast that he had never lost a boy, and I'm sure he never did. But every once in a while the Worcester *Gazette* reported drownings from canoes, especially at night. For us boys, a yearning to paddle the Lake at night succeeded our earlier longing to swim in it in the daytime. But for our mothers, the physical hazard of canoeing was almost eclipsed by their sense of its threat to chastity. One day, the whole street buzzed with scandal. Because of an evening in a canoe, one of our best-known young ladies had hastily to announce her engagement to a young man far below her in the Providence Street social scale. (The outsider might have thought that all Providence Street was fairly homogeneous as far as class distinction went, but he would have been wrong. Socially, it was as stratified as a geologic formation.) There was sufficient reason that the statement "He took her canoeing" had a knowing overtone of the illicit.

It was, therefore, a tremulous moment when you handed your girl off Coburn's rather rickety dock and she settled herself against the cushions while you masterfully seized the paddle in the back seat and shoved off. Across the Lake, the water mirrored resplendently the dazzling lights of the amusement park, White City, with its Ferris wheel, chute-the-chutes, and penny peep shows. You paddled past the merry-go-round on the near side as it churned out the "Poet and Peasant Overture," and presently von Suppé's rhythms competed with those of the dance-hall orchestra just beyond, which was probably playing a popular tune of the time, a song extolling the delights of travel on "The Old Fall River Line," the lyric of which conveyed the impression that for general indulgence the Fall River boats were no more than enlarged canoes. By the time you went under the Old Aqueduct, the sounds of the merry-go-round and the dance band had become faint and, ahead, the Lake opened out into darkness, mystery, and that unknown danger of which the Providence Street mothers were afraid.

At the time of my involvement with Miss Sears, these hazards were still well ahead of me. After my friend had made fun of me for having Miss Sears' photograph in my bedroom, my affair with her went underground. I went on gathering photographs and clippings of my heroine, but in secret.

I had photographs of Miss Sears getting on and off horses, sitting securely on them, and leaping fences. That there existed people who used horses merely for riding was in itself extraordinary, and it added greatly to the aura surrounding Miss Sears. Once, I am sure, she not only rode a horse but wore simultaneously a glittering silk hat of the kind we called "stovepipes." Stovepipes, as we knew them, were the hats rented by bridegrooms for public weddings in Horticultural Hall, on Front Street, an auditorium that was considered the last word for elegant Providence Street weddings. It had a highly polished floor, and before the ceremony we boys would skate madly about on it till we were stopped by our elders. An uncle of mine was married there, and I remember him in a long, rented frock coat and a stovepipe hat as he stood in position, enduring the protracted, rather sad service conducted in Hebrew.

One day, Miss Sears' life took on a new direction that brought her, in a moment of ecstatic amalgamation, close to me. She developed a new and unexpected talent, a potentiality of which she herself, perhaps, had only recently become aware. She had always ridden horses and played tennis and danced, but now she began to walk. The newspapers started to apply to her a strange, new word. She became what they reverently called a pedestrian. I carefully spelled the odd word out to myself and kept repeating it wonderingly on my walks to the Lake. I hadn't the faintest idea what it meant. I thought it must be the noun to designate some obscurely fashionable pastime that could be familiar only to those who lived in the realms inhabited by Miss Sears. For a long time, I did not connect the word in the newspaper headlines and under the photographs with the activities described in the articles that accompanied them.

In these articles, I read with amazement that Miss Sears, when she wanted to go to New York from Boston, disdained the Merchants' Limited and simply walked. She thought nothing, it appeared, of strolling from Newport to Montreal. The records of these extended walks filled columns in the Boston papers, and I took an intense pride in her mileage. And then, one day, as I was passing the Insane Asylum, there happened in my mind one of those instantaneous collocations which, I suppose, in loftier spheres have by quick mutation advanced the frontiers of philosophy and science. When the sportswriters or social column reporters said that Miss Sears was a pedestrian, they merely meant that she was a walker. Miss Sears and I were pedestrians together!

I began to multiply feverishly in my mind. Every day in summer, I walked eight miles—four miles to the Lake and four miles back. In two weeks, that made a hundred and twelve miles. That must be as far as from Boston to New York. Of course, Miss Sears did it all in a day or two, but after all, I consoled myself, she devoted her entire time to it. As soon as I discovered this community of interest between Miss Sears and myself, I no longer kept my infatuation for her a secret. I became quite brazen about her and flaunted our relationship. I carried my clippings in my pocket on the way to the Lake, showed them to the other boys, and compared my tallies with hers. At first, my companions were amused, and then scornful. One day, one of them taunted me. "Why don't you quit Worcester and walk to Boston and marry Miss Sears?" he asked.

"I don't intend to marry," I said with dignity, "but I think we can still be friends."

So odd is the course of destiny that this ambition was actually realized, at least for a few hours, on the occasion that I met Miss Sears for the first and last time. For within an hour after my Boston friend rang me up, I found myself in Miss Sears' drawing room, and there she was coming toward me to greet me. Her pedestrianism, as she crossed the room, met all my expectations; it was still elastic and lively. She was slim, tweedy, and, although her hair was gray, the whole impression she conveyed was youthful. Her eyes were very blue and very clear. She said that she was glad to see me. I told her at once that during my childhood in Worcester I had been, like her, a pedestrian. Miss Sears mistook, somehow, a past avocation for a present one.

195

"What was your last walk?" she asked, without beating about the bush.

I had just come from the Pacific Coast. I don't know what made me say it, unless I thought it would make Miss Sears smile. "Los Angeles to San Francisco," I told her.

"I've done it," said Miss Sears crisply. "How long did it take you?"

9

DOUBLE CHOCOLATE WITH

EMMA AND SASHA

The glow shed over my childhood by Miss Eleonora Sears was darkened by another figure, formidable and frightening. The power of the second was overwhelming and her shadow hovered over me until well into later life. Some time ago, in a review of an anthology of pieces from the *Little Review*, I was startled by the critic's characterization of Emma Goldman (some of whose letters from prison were reprinted in the book) as "that so different rebel." What startled me was the grotesqueness—to me, at least—of the understatement. The occasional reappearances of Emma in my

197

later life always unnerve me. The epithet applied to her during my childhood by my elders was so lethal, so searing, that it seemed to me impossible then that anyone could survive it—and yet Emma did. Some years ago, when I met Alla Nazimova at a party, she startled me even more than the understatement of the book review did by her calm declaration that she would like to do a play about Emma Goldman and play the part of Emma. My face must have registered my shock, because Miss Nazimova at once asked me whether I thought her idea was bad. I then had to explain to her that my dismay at her plan transcended any question of theatrical practicality; my reaction to it was in another realm entirely. It was, I told her, as if she had quietly announced her intention of playing Anti-Christ—or, more strictly, Anti-God—and I tried to convey to her the aura, at once mephitic and seductive, that surrounded Emma during my childhood.

One day, when I was still very young, Providence Street began to come alive with rumors and horrid allegations about the proprietors of a new ice-cream parlor that had been opened in our neighborhood. We children were forbidden to patronize the anathematized parlor, and it was a long time before I dared to defy the ban. Since the new entrepreneurs were Emma Goldman and Alexander Berkman (whom Miss Goldman called Sasha), some people might have disapproved of them on political grounds; the hatred of the

Providence Street parents was founded on religious ones. A dread word was applied to Miss Goldman —for somehow most of the vituperation focussed on her instead of on her consort and partner, Berkman, to whom, Providence Street whispered, she was not even married! Some idea of the virulence of the term used to describe Miss Goldman may be gathered from the fact that after the utterance of it the other accusation—that she and Berkman were not married—took on an aspect not so much of derogation as of amiable gossip. The epithet was the word *"apikorista,"* a word that to my elders connoted the ultimate in human depravity. An *apikoros—apikorista* was the feminine Yiddish form of this Hebrew word—was a renegade from the Jewish religion, but the word had the even deeper and more sinister connotation of treachery not merely to the Jewish religion but to God himself. That there existed such a person as an *apikorista* scarcely bore thinking about, and I remember distinctly the horror I felt when I heard the word used to describe a tangible, visible person who actually lived in and was doing business in our midst. I knew that there must be people who had defied God, because how otherwise could the word have come into existence, but here it was applied to a person whom one saw on the streets and who actually had a store within walking distance of one of the stricter synagogues. I remember telling Miss Nazimova that after thirty years or so I could not suppress a feeling of dismay that anyone, even an actress as boldly vital as she was, should express the wish, of her own free will and in public, to portray an out-and-out *apikorista!*

Although the word *"apikoros"* is Hebrew, it comes from the Greek *"Epikouros"* This is, of course, the name of the philosopher Epicurus, so that etymologically Emma was merely an Epicurean, which is not, in more liberal circles, a fighting word. It still takes considerable effort for me to realize that an *apikorista* is, after all, only a lady freethinker or skeptic. But these last are agreeable words; "freethinker" even has an implication of independence that is admirable. There must be a fierce history behind the assimilation into Hebrew of the Greek word, stemming from the ancient days when many Jews were seduced by the blandishments of the Greek philosophy of hedonism. The misinterpretation of Epicureanism as a philosophy of unbridled license no doubt led to a further identification of it with a defiance of God, and thus to the Hebrew religious formalists the word *"apikoros"* eventually became a symbol of the ultimate sin—atheism. Therefore, to be an *apikorista* was no laughing matter; the word carried such a weight of obloquy that it was applied only to those guilty of the most monstrous of human delinquencies. Providence Street first heard merely that Miss Goldman was an Anarchist, and we children repeated the news with scoffing ribaldry. I did not know what "Anarchist" meant, exactly, and to me the word had no more than a pleasant reverberation of wickedness. Even to my elders, it seemed to make Emma simply a figure of fun, for as a cult Anarchism had no adherents on Providence Street. But now my elders were calling her an *apikorista* as well, and where God was involved, the orthodox of Providence Street permitted no latitude.

I remember that before I ever saw Miss Goldman, I used to lie awake at night thinking about her fearfully and trying to imagine her appearance, which I am sure I must have invested with the traditional properties of diabolism. The thought that I might one day see her—pass her in the street—filled me with terror; I hoped that such a disastrous accident would not occur. She was an acute bogy, and even after she and Berkman left Worcester, impelled by their solemn decision to shoot Henry Glay Frick (which Emma describes in her autobiography, *Living My Life,* with that extraordinary, humorless intensity characteristic of saints and fanatics), her legend was perpetuated. The Providence Street parents cited her to us constantly, using her name somewhat as English parents used Napoleon's in the first decades of the nineteenth century, to frighten and to admonish. For the orthodox elders of the Providence Street synagogues, Alexander Berkman's attempt to assassinate Frick was a miraculous piece of luck. "What could you expect?" they demanded of us children, as if we were somehow subtly involved in the *attentat*, and as if they took it for granted we were all potential agnostics. ("*Attentat*" is a favorite word of Emma's, by the way, and it recurs throughout her autobiography. Webster defines it as "an attempt, especially an unsuccessful one, to commit a crime of violence.") "What could you expect of people who don't believe in God?" said our elders. "Naturally, such people are murderers!"

Finally, I met Emma Goldman. All my life I have told the same story of how it happened, and I told it that night to Alla Nazimova:

One day when I was grubbing in the cinders of the empty lot next to the Crompton & Knowles factory, on Winter Street, where I used to hunt for bits of glass and metal, I was picked up and walked home by Allie London. He was several years older than I, and I trudged along happily beside him.

"Where do you think I've been?" said Allie, with a kind of glowing, suppressed bravado.

I guessed the lake. I guessed Bancroft Tower.

Allie smiled at these conventional guesses. "I have just had a college ice"—late-nineteenth-century for sundae—"at Emma Goldman's," he announced sturdily.

I was aghast. I couldn't believe it. I stared at Allie, expecting that his appearance would have been somehow altered by the dread contact. Had there been incipient horns sprouting from his forehead, I would not have been surprised. But Allie looked about the same.

"How was it?" I finally managed to stammer.

"Wonderful!" said Allie enthusiastically. "She gives you a double helping for the same money. I'm not going to Elkind's any more."

"But I mean"—I could not bring myself to say the name—"*she?*"

Allie, an extrovert and already emancipated from orthodoxy, was impatient. "I tell you she gives you double. I asked for vanilla and she put on a scoop of strawberry, too. Same money."

I walked along beside Allie in a turmoil, convinced that by the necromancy of the extra scoop Emma had already begun to draw him into her coils.

"Did you see her?" I asked finally.

"Sure I saw her. She served me. Saw her feller, too. They had a fight. I could hear 'em in the back room. They're not married, you know. They had a whale of a fight."

This startled me. Up to then, I had thought that only married people fought. Under the circumstances, it seemed almost unfair for the Goldman-Berkman ménage to assume this prerogative of respectability.

A few days later, Allie again interrupted my excavations in Crompton & Knowles' cinder yard. "Want a treat?" he shouted cheerily.

Of course I did, but as I trotted along beside him, I was suddenly assailed by fear. "You taking me to Elkind's?" I asked hopefully.

"Not using Elkind's any more, I told you. I'm taking you to Goldman's. She gives you double. Don't know how she makes it pay, but that's her lookout."

It was also mine. I felt that my immortal soul hung in the balance. I whimpered. "Suppose my folks hear about it?"

"You don't believe that stuff, do you?" said Allie masterfully.

I have carried all my life a vivid impression of the subsequent scene in the ice-cream parlor. Berkman I do not seem to remember at all except for his voice, but I have always retained a clear picture of Miss Goldman—of her look of ineluctable benevolence, of her great mop of unruly red-blond hair, of her smile, and of her eyes, which I have always been sure were blue. I remember the shock of discovering that she was not frightening; it was my introduction, I have always believed, to the tangled world of reality, in which even the despised, the criminal, the fanatically wrongheaded, the hopelessly perverted may yet have a certain charm.

The counter was neat, and the benevolent deity stood behind it. When Allie asked me what I wanted, I was tongue-tied; I fully expected some emanation from the *apikorista* to pulverize me. Did she say, to temper Allie's impatience, "Take your time, my boy, there's no hurry"? I have always believed so. I managed finally to articulate a desire for chocolate. When it came—double scoop, twice what you would have got at Elkind's—Allie gave me the triumphant side glance of the successful prospector.

Miss Goldman left us, and we sat at the counter and ate. Soon, from the back room, came the lifted voices— Emma's and Berkman's. Allie looked at me significantly. "Fighting again," he whispered.

I have always flattered myself that I was more discerning than Allie that day. Though the voices were lifted, I sensed that it was not in anger or recrimination. The language they spoke was neither English nor Yiddish; the Yiddish I spoke at home and the English I spoke on the streets and in school were the two languages I knew, so I could not know that those loud words were Russian. But I sensed that there was no anger in the intonation; the discussion had the volume and the intensity of a quarrel but no animus. It was even sorrowful. I wondered. I wondered deeply.

When I got home, my sense of guilt was so profound that I was sure my mother would immediately see that I had done something wrong. But she didn't. I went to sleep that night with the pleasurable, lawless feeling that this was, after all, a world in which crime could go undetected. After that, I went to Emma's whenever Allie asked me. There were few excursions that could satisfy, simultaneously and so fully, a boy's natural instincts for the illicit and for the wholesome. It was like comfortably spooning up delicious ice cream in the Inferno. Nickels didn't come my way very often, and when I was not invited by Allie, I fell into the habit of wandering by the forbidden ice cream parlor in the hope that something would turn up. Nothing ever did. I even remember wondering whether, since Emma gave you a double scoop for one nickel, she might not be so quixotic as to give you one scoop for nothing. I never tested it out.

But whenever I did go into Emma's baleful precincts, I always heard the eternal chain argument from the back room. It went on and on, the voices rising and falling, intense without bitterness, violent without anger. One day, I got a nickel of my own, the gift of a prodigal uncle, and with it clutched in my palm I made at once for Emma's. To my consternation, the place was closed. I peered inside. The room was dismantled—chairs heaped one on top of the other. The kindly Devil and her voluble consort were gone. I turned away disconsolate. Without Mme. Mephistopheles, Worcester seemed less like Heaven than usual.

I discussed the vanished couple with Allie. His uncle was a friend of their landlord. Allie told me that to the landlord the sudden decision of his tenants to give up the parlor had seemed an act of pure insanity, for the place had been doing a land-office business in spite of the disapproval of Providence Street. Evidently the double scoops of ice cream had

paid off, for the profits were fabulous; they sometimes, said the landlord, came to fifty dollars a
week. (The standards of affluence in those days
were fairly modest; I remember that an uncle of
mine who was not on speaking terms with one of
his brothers denounced him to me one day, capping
his long complaint with the bitter remark "And
with all this he is a Croesus!" This surprised me; the
Croesus seemed as shabby and ineffectual as my
other uncles. I expressed my doubt. "Why," shouted
my uncle, "in the real estate alone he has four hundred dollars!") To give up a thriving business for no
reason, in the full tide of success, was unheard of on
Providence Street. "But what can you expect?" the
landlord said to Allie's uncle in final summary,
shrugging his shoulders. "What can you expect of
an *apikorista* who isn't even married?"

Everything about Emma's legend was shocking, but
the greatest shock of all was to come when, after
telling Miss Nazimova my story, which all my life I
had devoutly believed, I was impelled to read
Emma's autobiography. From it I discovered that
Emma had been in business in Worcester in 1892, in
the months immediately preceding the shooting of
Frick, and that just prior to the attempted assassina-
tion she and Berkman had left Worcester, never to
return. Now, I have always written in my passport
applications that I was born in 1893, but it is a facti-

tious date, because I have never known my actual birth date. The reason for this lamentable ignorance is as follows: My father entered all our births as they occurred—my two brothers', my sister's, and mine—in Hebrew on the inside back cover of one of his volumes of the Talmud. Since he figured our births according to the Hebrew calendar, this automatically gave me a three-thousand-year jump on my contemporaries. Even as a child, this made me feel superannuated, but there wasn't much I could do about it. I let it pass; the task of translating the date into a more contemporary system was too complicated. There came a day, though, when this archaic computation of my father's was to cause me acute embarrassment. It happened during class at the Providence Street School, when our teacher, probably because she was unable to find my age in her records, took it into her head to ask me suddenly when I was born. I discovered, equally suddenly, that I didn't know. I didn't answer, and she repeated the question, somewhat sharply. I couldn't risk telling the truth—that I didn't know my birthday. I was ashamed to confess it before the whole class, so I quickly improvised one. "June," I heard myself saying. "June what?" the teacher demanded. "June 9th," I said. The teacher must have felt that she was dealing with a congenital idiot. "The year?" she said wearily. "Do you mind telling me the year?" "Eighteen-ninety-three," I stammered, picking what seemed like a good one.

This improvisation became fixed; it has served as well as any other, and until I read Emma Goldman's autobiography it did not trouble me that it made little pretension to accuracy. I have long since forgotten the Hebrew date of my birth, and my father's many-volume Talmud was long ago given away, so I cannot look up that recording and translate it into a date in our calendar. I have made several attempts to get the official date of my birth from the City of Worcester, but without success; there is no record there of my ever having been born. But common sense tells me that 1893 must be reasonably close. I graduated from high school in 1911, and if I had been born early enough to remember visiting Emma Goldman's ice-cream parlor, I would have been well over twenty when I graduated. This seems unlikely, since I always appeared to be about the same age as my classmates. I can only regretfully conclude that my meeting with Emma never happened. My older brothers certainly grew up sniffing the effluvium of Emma's reputation, and it seems probable that I appropriated their memories of her for my own. Did I materialize the lurid gossip about Emma, which threaded Providence Street like a contaminated brook long after she had left Worcester, into a personal experience and annex the *apikorista* into my private mythology? It seems probable. I certainly dreamed about her—a female Devil without horns but with suitably flaming hair. My memory of her is so vivid that I still see that tousled head, hear that argument, and taste that double chocolate. But I now reluctantly accept the fact that all these years I must have been experiencing these things at second hand.

It was only when I read Emma's autobiography that I discovered that she and Berkman gave up their ice cream business in Worcester not because they were skeptics but because they were fanatical believers. I nurtured for years the little mystery of the high-voiced arguments in the back room; when I came to read Emma's autobiography, I solved it. Emma and Sasha had decided that America was too materialistic for the revolution; it became clear to them that by accelerating a revolution in Russia they might create a model for one here. To get the money for the trip to Russia, they drifted to Worcester and set up the ice-cream parlor. Business flourished; they were practically on their way. One day, a customer, while eating his ice cream, was reading a paper. Emma's roving eye caught the headline: "LATEST DEVELOPMENTS IN HOMESTEAD—FAMILIES OF STRIKERS EVICTED FROM THE COMPANY HOUSES—WOMAN IN CONFINEMENT CARRIED OUT INTO STREET BY SHERIFFS" Emma, as she herself tells it, made an instant deal with the man. She told him that he could have his ice cream free if he would let her read his paper. Then she ran to Sasha with the news. The project to go to Russia was abandoned; it was supplanted by the more immediate necessity of getting rid of the tyrant of Homestead—Henry Clay Frick. There follows Emma's description of a protracted argument: Should *she* go or should *he* go? There was no doubt in Berkman's mind that he should go; Emma agreed to this but insisted that she must accompany him. No, said Sasha; she had a gift for words, a knack for propaganda. He must go to Pittsburgh and deal with Frick personally, and Emma must remain behind to tell about it. The argument went on for a long time, and Emma sorrowfully describes how she lost it.

Emma then tells of the astonishment of the landlord, Allie's uncle's friend, when she told him they were giving up the business. They gave him that day's receipts as a settlement for back rent—seventy-five dollars—and took the next train to New York. The subsequent events are grimly and fantastically farcical, though Emma appears to have had no glimmering of that. They at once set about manufacturing a bomb. On this task, Sasha promptly wasted forty dollars, because he appears to have had no knack for bomb-making. But the impulse for a rendezvous with Mr. Frick was so imperious that Sasha left for Pittsburgh anyway. Emma remained behind in New York, and decided that in order to aid Sasha with money she would become a streetwalker—an avocation for which she seems to have had as little aptitude as Sasha had for bomb-making. The only man who picked her up was an elderly intellectual, who gave her ten dollars and ran away in panic at her suggestion that perhaps she ought to earn it. Meanwhile, in Pittsburgh, Berkman had managed to buy a cheap revolver. Gun in hand, he strolled into Frick's private office (how accessible those early tycoons must have been!) and shot him. He failed to kill him, but he wounded him seriously. Emma immediately started organizing mass meetings to celebrate the *attentat*. But when Frick refused to die, there was much sneering and head-shaking in Anarchist circles in New York. Emma's inspiration in Anarchy had been a well-known revolutionary editor of the time named Johann Most. In fact, Emma writes that it was from Most's book *Science of Revolutionary Warfare* that Sasha, a tyro, had got his first shy hints about bomb-making. It "was a good textbook," says Emma. Now, to Emma's profound disgust, Most's paper, *Freiheit*, came out with an article denouncing the attack on Frick. Aspersions were cast on Berkman's motives. There was even a suggestion that he had shot Frick with a toy revolver and that that was why Frick was still alive. This slander aroused Emma's fierce indignation:

> I was stung to the quick. I knew that Sasha had never had much practice in shooting. Occasionally, at German picnics, he would take part in target-shooting, but was that sufficient? I was sure that Sasha's failure to kill Frick was due to the cheap

quality of his revolver—he had lacked enough money to buy a good one.

She has another explanation to cover Sasha's inefficiency:

> Perhaps Frick was recovering because of the attention he was getting? The greatest surgeons of America had been called to his bedside. Yes, it must be that; after all, three bullets from Sasha's revolver had lodged in Frick's body. It was Frick's wealth that was enabling him to recover. I tried to explain this to the comrades, but most of them remained unconvinced. Some even hinted that Sasha was at liberty. I was frantic—how dared they doubt Sasha? I would write him! I would ask him to send me word that would stop the horrible rumors about him.

In any case, by not dying Frick blurred the impact of Berkman's act.

Emma has the engaging habit, in her autobiography, of putting a summarizing running head at the top of each page. These heads are extremely diverting and various; by merely following them, without reading the text beneath, you may quickly get a running record of a lively career. For example:

I Divorce My Husband
I Remarry Kershner [her husband] and Leave Him
   Again
My Doubts About Nihilism Disappear
Johann Most: Preceptor
I Dedicate Myself to Most's Happiness

I Advocate Free Love
I am Drawn to Sasha
I Give Myself to Sasha
I Respond to Fedya

The last two heads run on facing pages. Then come:

I Belong Entirely to Sasha
I Plan My First Lecture Tour
Most Confesses Love for Me
Most Wants Merely the Female
Sasha Plus Most Equals Fedya
I Refuse to Bear Children
Most Stirs Me Profoundly
"Love, Love—There Is Only Sex!"
Blackwell's Island Claims Most
Sasha Plans an Attentat
  —and Insists on Executing It Alone
I Find Love in the Arms of Ed
Ed Shows a Conservative Streak
I Leave Ed
My Reactions to Procreation Among the Poor
The President [McKinley] Dies. Am I Sorry?
We Must Try to Help Czolgosz
I Long for Ben Reitman
Despite His Defects, I Love Ben
I Worry About My Face
Billy Sunday Nauseates Me

And so on and on. The pages on which Emma describes her disillusion with Most's attitude about Berkman's sacrifice is headed simply "I Horsewhip

Johann Most."

In 1919, Emma and Sasha were deported for criminal Anarchy. Thanks to the insistent courtesy of the United States Government, they had free passage to their beloved Russia. Just before entering Russia, after crossing Finland locked in a train, with sentries with fixed bayonets inside the cars and on the platforms, Emma writes, "My heart trembled with anticipation and fervent hope." Almost as soon as she and Sasha reached Moscow and got the hang of things in their utopia, their disenchantment began. In swift montage, Emma's headings give a capsule history of her Russian visit:

We Are Dazzled by the Results in Russia
I Begin to Wonder
Jack Reed Bursts in on Me
I Will Not Believe What I See
Tyranny in Russia
Lenin Sends for Sasha and Me
Lenin Talks to Us
Russia Lies Fallow
I Clash with Soviet Officials
We Get Comrades out of Jail
Misery in the Factories
Suspicious Bertrand Russell
Lenin, the False Messiah
My Disillusionment Persists
"The Revolution, What Has Become of It?"
Respect for Human Life: A Rarity
The Bolshevik Myth

Emma left Russia on December 1, 1921. On the train, she writes, "My dreams crushed, my faith broken, my heart like a stone. *Matuska Rossiya* [Mother Russia] bleeding from a thousand wounds, her soil strewn with the dead. I clutch the bar at the frozen windowpane and grit my teeth to suppress my sobs."

Emma must have been among the first in the long procession of the disillusioned.

10

MR. WOLFSON'S STAINED-GLASS WINDOW

The Croesus of Providence Street was Mr. Wolfson. He lived in a mud-colored concrete villa. Several of the richer Providence Street residents had houses of which they occupied half. These were double wooden houses with a separate stoop and entrance for each family. But Mr. Wolfson's mansion of puckered concrete was all his own. It was a house around which one could build dreams. It had a turret and irrational wings and a massive front door with curtained glass panels at each side and a polished brass electric push button, like a doctor's. Concrete bat-

217

tlements pierced by alternate square and diamond-shaped apertures circled the roof. But the magic and the wonder of Mr. Wolfson's mansion was that it had, instead of the customary parlor windows, with their lace curtains on brass rods, a great, darkly resplendent oval of stained glass. The room with the oval window was itself oval in shape and it had in it an upright piano. The Wolfsons always referred to it proudly as "the music room." Neither of them played the piano and it is unlikely that they knew much about music; nevertheless, they were secure in the possession of the only music room on the hill. Mr. Wolfson's house, with its stained-glass window, was the show place of Providence Street. It never occurred to any of us to wonder what effect this multi-colored jewel had on the light in Mr. Wolfson's parlor. We never reflected that the room might be gloomy; nothing about Mr. Wolfson could be anything but iridescent. He moved majestically up and down the hill in a nimbus of spectacular opulence.

Providence Street always referred to Mr. Wolfson as the *Gvirr*. A *Gvirr* was what we should now call a tycoon. Many Providence Street businessmen were referred to as *Gvirrim*, but Mr. Wolfson was, indisputably, *the Gvirr*. I remember hushed speculations about the extent of his fortune, ranging from bearish mutters of fifty thousand dollars to the flamboyant estimates of the bulls, who pronounced confidently that Mr. Wolfson must be worth two hundred thousand— probably because they enjoyed giving utterance to a figure so astronomical. Actually, it did not require much wealth on Providence Street to belong to the class of the *Gvirrim*. The term was applied somewhat loosely.

Because he was the richest man in our community, Mr. Wolfson was appointed by the Mayor of Worcester a City Marshal. In this honorary office, his duty was entirely ornamental; he led parades. He bought a white horse and had special riding boots and breeches made to his measure. Mounted on his white horse and jaunty in his riding habiliments, he would course down Providence Street of a Sunday morning. From the eminence of his saddle he would look down on the little businessmen, his acquaintances rather than his friends, with a jeering expression, because they were not, like himself, equestrians. This did not enhance his popularity.

Of all the Providence Street celebrities of my childhood, I can now see Mr. Wolfson the most clearly. I remember his sartorial elegance. In a community that, on weekdays, was not too meticulous about collars and ties, he was always sprucely dressed. He was a shortish, sallow man, with a militant, ginger-colored mustache, the ends of which he was always sharpening between thumb and forefinger, and he had ginger-colored

219

hair, parted in the middle. His eyes, too, were yellowish—ophidian, incessantly darting about, with a look at once furtive and arrogant. He was a comb manufacturer, and he was the color of one of his own imitation-amber combs. I never remember seeing Mr. Wolfson smile; he was always grim. But since our lives in those days focussed in the Providence Street Synagogue, and since Mr. Wolfson, after an intense and scandalous campaign, became for a season its president, I remember him best as he was on Friday nights and Saturdays and high holidays, wearing the presidential regalia and sitting in state in a special armchair beside the Ark, opposite the rabbi. On these occasions, Mr. Wolfson wore a stovepipe silk hat, a Prince Albert coat, and striped trousers. The fabulous circumstance was that he owned these garments outright. In this, he was unique; in our circle, such garments were nearly always hired, and seldom used except for weddings.

I remember Mrs. Wolfson, too. She was a large, handsome woman and she had, in contrast to her husband, a benign air. Once, Mrs. Wolfson went to Boston and came back in a new tweed suit. This suit was a nine days' wonder. Such a fabric as tweed had never appeared in our neighborhood before. The Wolfsons were the first people on Providence Street to own a car. It was a Winton Six. I remember being awakened, early on a sum-

mer morning, by a chum with the information
that Mrs. Wolfson was going to Boston in her car.
We ran up the hill and, sure enough, there was
Mrs. Wolfson, in a straw hat and veil, a little
Gioconda smile on her lips, getting into her car to
be driven off to her summer holiday at Revere
Beach, a resort near Boston. It seemed to me then
that Mr. Wolfson, leading his wife to the Winton
Six as they were about to start on their outing,
represented all that an Alger hero could achieve
in one lifetime.

The Wolfsons were childless. As there was
much jealousy of them even before the scandal
over the coveted presidency, there were many
standard, and ribald, jokes about this fact, most of
which I did not then understand. Providence
Street took its revenge for Mr. Wolfson's opulence
by reflecting on his infertility. It was not only the
Wolfsons' wealth that made the gossip about
them so invidious; it was also their social isola-
tion. *Their* friends were all in Boston. They went
constantly to see people in Boston; people from
Boston came to see them. Once even a banker
from Toronto came and brought his daughter. The
Wolfsons, we awesomely thought, must have
extra bedrooms for house guests. Neither my parents nor any of their friends ever visited the
Wolfsons socially; they were never asked. I suppose that, like the Duke in Max Beerbohm's
Zuleika Dobson, Mr. Wolfson felt that there was

simply no one on Providence Street qualified to join the Junta composed of himself and his wife. Some of our mothers occasionally got into the Wolfson house, though, when they went to solicit money for charity drives. They were always received by Mrs. Wolfson, who interviewed them graciously in the music room behind the stained-glass window. The visitors never went away empty-handed, but they invariably got the sense that their stay must terminate automatically with the bestowal of a check.

The scandal over Mr. Wolfson's accession to the presidency of the synagogue was a *cause célèbre* of my childhood. It would be difficult to convey to what degree the mental and spiritual life of Providence Street was obsessed by the idea of the importance of learning. I do not refer to secular education but to theological. An oligarchy, zealous and austere, dominated the intellectual circles of Providence Street, and its shibboleth was a knowledge of the Sacred Books. With a kind of jocular awe, it would be said of a man of learning, "He knows his Black Dots!" This subtle and heady praise was reserved for the massive scholars, the truly erudite. The Black Dots were periods placed singly or in slanting rows under the letters in the sacred chants—the "Song of Songs," for example—and were musical notations for

222

their cantillation. A man's standing in the intellectual life of the community was determined, symbolically, by his familiarity with the Black Dots. My father belonged to a group whose avocation it was to read through the six basic Talmudic books of the Mishna once a year. Avocation is hardly the word, since, for the members of this group, it was their outside, worldly lives that were marginal, not their religious absorptions. They spoke in hushed reverence of the great scholars of Russia—the saints, or *Gaonim,* as they were called—who read the entire sixty volumes of the Talmud once a year. In this task, the scholars were assisted by the circumstance that they knew most of the Talmudic books by heart anyway. But on Providence Street, the learned sect contented itself with reading through the six volumes of the Mishna.

Just as the phrase "He knows his Black Dots" was the accolade of grace, so another phrase connoted the ultimate in vituperation. This was to say of a man, "He is a *Grober Jung* [Gross Fellow]!" It is impossible to convey, in a literal translation from the Yiddish, the virulent contempt of this expression. You might have written the English prose of a Walter Pater, but on Providence Street, if you were unfamiliar with theological law, the endless convolutions of Talmudic exegesis, you were a Gross Fellow and there was nothing to be done about it; spiritually and intellectually you were in limbo. You might have got rich by manufacturing combs, you might have a Winton Six, a tweedy wife, a stained-glass window, and connections in Boston and Toronto, but to the Sanhedrin, who were the uncrowned dictators of the intense spiritual and mental life of the hill, if you weren't on speaking terms with the Black Dots, you were out of the running. The epithet *Grober Jung* conveyed a density not merely intellectual but spiritual, a coarseness of sensibility as well as opacity of mind. It sometimes amused me when it was applied by coarse fellows to others no less coarse, but the shot always told.

Now, Mr. Wolfson knew nothing at all about the Black Dots. He was, by common consent, a *Grober Jung.* I have thought since that if I had then known the phrase "inferiority complex," I might have used it to explain Mr. Wolfson and I have felt that it was the menace of the, to him, unknown Black Dots that did him in. Mr. Wolfson, it is clear to me now, must have had an intense awareness of his intellectual shortcomings. Perhaps he thought to compensate for them by acquiring the glittering bauble of the presidency of the Providence Street Synagogue, which had become vacant. In any case, Mr. Wolfson threw his hat into the ring. (Did he argue, I wonder, that at least he had the wardrobe for it?) His first move was to endow a Hebrew school for the young. There was no rabbinical Hatch Act to limit campaign expenditure, and Mr. Wolfson spent lavishly. The street buzzed with controversy and indignation. An ignoramus who had not even a bowing acquaintance with the Black Dots to be president! A manifest Gross Fellow for president! An illiterate comb manufacturer to sit beside the Ark, dominating the congregation and on an equal eminence with the learned and revered Rabbi Silver himself! It was unthinkable, it was blasphemous, it was obscene. Nevertheless, Mr. Wolfson won.

The first Friday night that Mr. Wolfson, in full regalia, walked down the aisle to the presidential chair, the atmosphere of the Providence Street Synagogue was quivering with tension. The cognoscenti focussed on the majestically advancing figure looks of hostility and contempt. One could hear a faint sigh of disapprobation. I remember a fascinating item of Mr. Wolfson's inaugural costume; with the stovepipe hat and the Prince Albert and the striped trousers I was familiar, but for this occasion the incoming president had provided himself with an extraordinary tie, the like of which I had never seen. It was not a tie, properly speaking, at all. It was a little, puffed-out bed of shiny gray silk or satin, which entirely covered the triangle formed in the silk-faced lapels of Mr. Wolfson's coat. From the center of this coverlet, there gleamed a diamond pin. The new president mounted the carpeted steps to the little platform slowly, and before he sat down, he looked for a moment with defiance at the congregation, his dull, shifty eyes seeking out his enemies. His look plainly said, "You may be the master of the Black Dots, of which I know nothing, but I am master of you!" His glance swept for a moment to the gallery, where the ladies were segregated, and met his wife's. It seemed to me that they exchanged a look of mutual triumph. Then Mr. Wolfson gave a screw to his mustaches and sat down. I looked up at Mrs. Wolfson and was dazzled. She had seldom gone to the synagogue on Friday nights (her absence from these services had constituted the basis of one of the charges of impiety against the Wolfsons), but she was there that night to witness her husband's victory. I had never before seen Mrs. Wolfson in the evening, and I remember getting a clear impression that on this occasion she looked like an opera singer. She was ample, and I must have compared her, unconsciously, with colored posters of Tetrazzini at which I had stopped to stare in a record-shop window on Main Street.

The pride of office went to Mr. Wolfson's head and he eventually overplayed his hand. He must have been president for about six months and in the full tide of his power when an incident occurred that shook the street. One Saturday, during an interlude in the service, Mr. Wolfson did an unforgivable thing. He looked across the dais at Rabbi Silver and beckoned him to come over to the president's throne. I was standing beside my father, not far away, and saw the whole thing, as I was afterward called upon frequently to recount. Rabbi Silver, in response to the president's gesture, smiled but did not move. He shook his head slightly. He meant to convey to Mr. Wolfson that it was not becoming for a parishioner to summon a rabbi, no matter how exalted the parishioner was. Mr. Wolfson motioned again, and Rabbi Silver smiled and shook his head again. For a moment, the little strip of carpet between Mr. Wolfson and Rabbi Silver became a charged field—a Canossa.

The incident might have passed without too many repercussions, because Rabbi Silver was a wise and tolerant man, had it not been for the dramatic intrusion of Mr. Rubinstein, the Providence Street drunk. Mr. Rubinstein was a little, watery-eyed, grizzled old man, who fascinated me because he was nearly always talking to himself; whenever you met him, he was likely to be engaged in a deep and engrossing conversation with himself, and he did not mind in the least if you eavesdropped. Sometimes Mr. Rubinstein had to be refused admittance to the synagogue, but on the day of the little drama of Mr. Wolfson and Rabbi Silver, Mr. Rubinstein was present, and in a state of comparative lucidity. Since he did not happen to be interviewing himself that day, he was able to register what seemed to him an unforgivable lapse of form on Mr. Wolfson's part. He lurched up to the foot of the steps leading to the presidential chair and shouted up to Mr. Wolfson, shaking a fist at him, "How dare you! You ignoramus, how dare you motion to the Rabbi to come to a Gross Fellow like you! If you want him, there he is. Go to him, and thank your God he speaks to you!" Mr. Rubinstein uttered the dread *"Grober Jung"* so loudly that the whole congregation heard it. Mr. Wolfson's habitual pallor deepened. The spasmodic working of his cheek muscles revealed that the barbed epithet had reached its mark. He became suddenly pitiful. He wilted. True, the insult had come from the scum of the earth, but Mr. Wolfson was only too aware that it represented the communal opinion of him. I got a quick, undefined impression that it represented Mr. Wolfson's secret appraisal of himself. The dread thing had been blurted out loud; it could not be recalled. For a few days, the despised Mr. Rubinstein became a hero, the spokesman of the spirit against the fleshpots.

From then on, things went from bad to worse for Mr. Wolfson. To be sure, he finished out his term of office. He continued to wear his Prince Albert, and his stovepipe hat, he still twirled his mustache, but his eminence had become the eminence of the pillory. The virtuosi of the Black Dots jeered at him openly. He did not seek re-election, he no longer appeared in the synagogue, and he disappeared from my view and from the view of Providence Street generally. One day Providence Street munched with relish the rumor that Mr. Wolfson was "in trouble." His comb business had failed. His factory, it was said, had been taken over by the bank. These reports meant little to me. I still used to pass Mr. Wolfson's house and gape at his stained-glass window. No one who inhabited such grandeur, I was certain, could really be said to be in serious trouble. It was not until I learned that the bank had taken over Mr. Wolfson's house and had dispossessed him that I got a true inkling of the tragedy. For a long time after that, I kept passing the house. It looked mournful. The windows, except for the stained-glass one, were boarded up. Either the custodians from the bank were aesthetes or the size and shape of the oval window presented a mechanical problem they were too lazy to solve.

I was to see Mr. Wolfson just once more. It was a late afternoon in October of the next year. Coming back from a tramp in the woods beyond the Academy, I picked up Mr. Rubinstein. He was swaying along, deeply absorbed in one of his rapt conversations. He made no acknowledgment that I had joined him, but he must have been aware of it, because when he made what he apparently considered a good point, he nudged me and gave me a sly, self-appreciative glance out of the corners of his rheumy eyes. As we came to the

Wolfson mansion, I stopped. The setting sun had caught the stained-glass window and it glittered in a bewildering medley of color. Mr. Rubinstein, involved in his own dialectic, did not look at the window; he had stopped because I had, and he stood at the curb, his back to the house, summing up his case. As I turned regretfully away from the glory of Mr. Wolfson's window, I became aware of a nondescript figure toiling up the hill, on the opposite sidewalk. Suddenly, Mr. Rubinstein saw him, too; he forgot, for a moment, his personal argument and took time out to spout his automatic epithet at Mr. Wolfson. His voice rose in a kind of scream. "There he goes, the Gross Fellow!" he shouted.

It really was Mr. Wolfson. I should not have known him. He was tieless and collarless; his worn suit hung limply on his shrunken figure. His ginger mustache drooped forlornly. He saw us and, suddenly energized, started swiftly across the street toward us. As he came closer, I saw that his eyes, fastened on Mr. Rubinstein, were maniacal; he was riven with hatred. He howled something at Mr. Rubinstein, who had already forgotten him and had resumed his earlier argument with himself or, for all I knew, started another, entirely different. From the way Mr. Wolfson looked at him, I saw that Mr. Rubinstein symbolized for him the whole course of his downfall. I was sure that Mr. Wolfson was going to kill Mr.

Rubinstein. Indeed, halfway across the road, Mr. Wolfson bent down and picked up a rock to hurl at Mr. Rubinstein. I remember being horribly certain that if Mr. Wolfson missed Mr. Rubinstein, the rock would smash the stained-glass window, and, curiously, my concern was divided equally between the beloved window and Mr. Rubinstein. Mr. Wolfson advanced, rock in hand, murderous. At this moment, something pathetic must have cropped up in Mr. Rubinstein's talk with his imaginary interlocutor. He was completely unaware of Mr. Wolfson's approach; he had forgotten him entirely, and the new and unguessable situation he had become involved in was so poignant that he sat down suddenly on the curb and began to cry. Mr. Wolfson advanced. I wanted to explain to Mr. Wolfson that Mr. Rubinstein was lost in a labyrinth of his own, I wanted to stop him somehow, but I was paralyzed with irresolution. So, now, was Mr. Wolfson. It is probable that the sad story it suddenly occurred to Mr. Rubinstein to tell himself saved his life, for Mr. Wolfson must have misinterpreted Mr. Rubinstein's tears as a plea for mercy. The rock dropped from Mr. Wolfson's hand. He came up to Mr. Rubinstein and pushed him with his foot. Mr. Rubinstein rolled over comfortably on his side, still weeping contentedly. For a moment, Mr. Wolfson looked down at him with dead eyes. Then he resumed his climb up the hill.

A month or so later, when I passed the Wolfson house again, it was covered with scaffolding, and workmen were going in and out the front door. The bank was converting the house into tenements. Where the stained-glass window had been, there was now a gaping, oval eye. No revolution since—neither the crash in Wall Street nor the overturn in Russia nor the ebbing away of capitalism—has ever given me such a quick and vivid sense of mutability as the mournful disappearance of Mr. Wolfson's stained-glass window.

11

POINT OF THE NEEDLE

As I look back on my school days in Worcester, in the Providence Street grade school at the start of the century, and later in the Classical High School, I can see that these contemporary institutions were rather ineffectual in combatting the sombre fascination of the medievalism of my home. There we were—my parents, my two older brothers, and I—a family uprooted from a veiled and ancient and unhappy past, and plumped down, unaccountably, in the tenement district of an industrial city in New England. The American myths I acquired in my school history books— George Washington and the cherry tree, and the others—were thin and anemic compared to the

Biblical exploits I heard about at home. My father related the Old Testament stories as if they had taken place recently—as if they constituted his personal past.

How he had managed such a feat as to make the long journey from Lithuania to Worcester was a matter of endless speculation for me, and I constantly tried to delve into it, but with only fragmentary results. There was simply no relation between my father's world and the contemporary one. The streets of Worcester, my life with my playmates, the themes I studied at school were all marginal exercises. The Great Theme was at home, and it concerned God and the thick-textured history of the Jewish people. It was dark, fear-ridden, and oppressive, but it had the warmth and tenderness of companionship in a common danger. For all its fascination, it bred in me an acute longing to escape and shake off those extra centuries my father had added to my life the moment I was born.

This escape for which I longed so passionately was provided for me—in part, at least—by the lucky accident of my intimacy with Willie Lavin. As I look back on it now, the pains Willie took with me pass all credence. When I first began to write—this was not until I was about fifteen —he went over all my manuscripts, analyzing them, correcting them, and taking endless trouble to prepare them for submission to, and, of course, eventual rejection by, various publications.

234

During all these years there was no intellectual problem, no practical dilemma, no psychological crisis at home that I did not dump in Willie's lap. He became, so to say, my liaison officer between the medievalism of our household and the latter-day world; he understood both worlds, and he enjoyed trying to reconcile them for me.

During all these years, Willie himself was very busy, first as a student at the Worcester Polytechnic Institute, where he made an excellent record, and later as a chemist at the Worcester Water Works. While he was employed by the city, he decided to study law, and he did it by commuting to Boston four evenings a week to attend law school at Boston University. He got his degree in three years and passed the bar exams.

I don't know how Willie explained his preoccupation with me to his contemporaries, but he explained it to me by saying that it was "a question of planes." He adored my brothers and his other friends, he said, but he moved with them on a different plane from the one he shared with me. They were wonderful fellows, but Willie found them, as he put it, "a bit excessively down to earth." He said he couldn't discuss with them the things he discussed with me—abstract questions, for instance. I gathered also that I was a more patient listener than my brothers and their friends. Of course, I was young enough to have nothing to do but listen, whereas Willie's older friends all had jobs and were absorbed in their own lives.

So long as we children observed the ritualistic pieties—and these were fairly exacting—my father overflowed with loving-kindness toward us. But he did sternly forbid us two exercises: we were not to try under any circumstances to discover the true name of the Lord; we were not to think about the problem of infinity. It is unlikely that I would have done much speculation in either of these areas if I had not been so explicitly forbidden. In the first, I would have accepted as sufficient for my needs the various names of the Lord I heard in common use around the house—Adonai, Elohim, Adoshem, Melech Haolom, and Ribono Shel Olom—but these, my father said, were mere pseudonyms. They were names, not the Name. This I must never try to discover, for in it lay coiled the ultimate, pent-up sunburst of truth. And unless I was prepared to receive this truth—a preparation achieved only by the rarest of saints—the mere fact of approaching it, the faintest hint of what it was, might be instantly pulverizing. He said that even some of the saints, men who had spent their lives delving for the Name and had led lives of purity and piety in order to be ready to receive it, had, in approaching the split second of revelation, been atomized—not, I understood, because of any impurity in them but because of their arrogance in believing that they deserved to know. The Name was the final kernel of knowledge and to possess it was to be destroyed.

My father also warned me that it was especially hazardous and reprehensible to try to ambush the Name by resorting to black magic and the occult arts. He cautioned me as sombrely and literally as if Providence Street were teeming with such diabolical opportunities. Actually, among my pals on the hill I encountered neither abortive saintliness nor thaumaturgy. When I brought up the subject of the Name with my friends, I was amazed to find how little curiosity they had about it—with the exception of Willie, of course. The boys of my own age seemed to be more than satisfied with the names of the Lord that were current, and even a bit jaded about them.

My father really worried unnecessarily; the data at my disposal for making so lethal a discovery were rather scarce, my curiosity had little to feed on, and in general I obeyed his prohibition against excessive research. I did experience a certain terror of inadvertently stumbling on the dread Name, by overhearing it, perhaps, or seeing it written in letters of fire in a dream—a dream from which I would never wake up. However, my fears were groundless, too; no intimation ever reached me, nor did the representative of any occult society suggest that I take part in illicit experiment. The only magicians I saw were at Poli's Vaudeville Theatre and they were engaged in less abstract exhibitions. The principal effect of my father's prohibition was to induce my resentment, for it seemed to contradict the exhortations I was receiving constantly in school, and from my education-ravished elders at home (including my father), to pursue knowledge inexorably and wholeheartedly. If the ultimate molecule of truth resided in the hidden name of the Lord, and if I was forbidden to seek it, what was the use of slaving over grammar and arithmetic? School seemed a waste of time altogether. This gave me a convenient excuse on lovely spring days to play hooky and walk to the lake or, in autumn, to escape to Newton Hill and hunt for chestnuts.

My father's second injunction—not to think about infinity—gave me considerable trouble. Infinity involved the perpetually receding end of things. Here we were, my father and I, at a fixed point in space—31 Providence Street, Worcester, Massachusetts. Above us was the visible sky. Above the sky, there was space, which went on endlessly through an unimaginable number of remoter skies. To use the word "endlessly" was in itself a verbal evasion, because it wasn't possible to imagine anything without an end. And yet it was equally impossible to imagine space as finite. This was indeed a dilemma. Those who thought about infinity too much, my father solemnly warned me, usually went insane. "Therefore," he always said in conclusion, "you must not think about it!" But I could see that he himself was pondering it. Vainglorious, I suggested that perhaps one might, one day, with sufficient concentration, get to the bottom of it. My father shook his head. The problem was not for mortals to think about, still less to solve, and the penalty for solution was identical to that attendant on discovering the true name of the Lord—instant annihilation.

Lying in bed at night, I found myself engaged in formidable engineering projects, constructing arbitrary terminals for the eons of space—high ramparts, nonporous to the invading tide of infinity. But, tremendous as these barriers were, my imagination leaped them, as did space itself. Space must, I thought desperately, be put a stop to; it couldn't be allowed to run on forever. Yet it did. What *was* forever? One couldn't imagine it, but one had to if one was to tackle the subject at all. "Forever" was a term in time, yet it could also be applied to the limitlessness of space. It was very bewildering. In an effort to compromise with space, to be reasonable with it, I decided to give it all the scope it wanted—trillions and trillions of miles—in the hope that somewhere it would call a halt. But it always wanted more. Wrestling with space gave me a headachy feeling; it made me toss about in bed at night; it was maddening. That was what my father must have meant when he forbade me to think about the problem at all. But I couldn't stop. I thought about it sitting in classes at school, when I should have been listening to my teachers.

Finally, wearied of these agonies of cerebration, I

reached a point where I knew I couldn't bear it alone; I needed help. So one summer day when I was trudging to the lake for a swim with a boy named Freddie Eisenberg, I introduced the subject. Freddie was the star pupil of my class and an acknowledged intellectual. Appropriately enough, I put the dilemma before him while we were passing the insane asylum on Shrewsbury Street. Freddie was unsympathetic. He shrugged the whole thing off in an unaccountably callous manner. "I'll worry about *that* after we get to Jerry Daly's bathhouse," he said. "That's space enough for me!"

Since I couldn't whip up any interest in these pressing problems among friends of my own years, I was forced to take them to Willie. They were right up his alley. The day I brought up the subject of space and time, he invited me into Easton's for a milk shake, and there he met infinity head on. While he didn't, as I remember, actually solve the problem, he diminished it, somehow, by multiplying it. He didn't in any way duck the issue, but he widened the area and shifted the field; he relegated it to its proper place by revealing it as only one thread in the fabric of a larger mystery. Willie had a way of starting his discussions with impressive phrases: "I can well imagine a situation where . . ." "I venture the opinion that . . ." "I will go so far as to say that . . ." "Let us begin by reducing the problem to its component parts . . ." Or he would say, "There is no problem that will not yield to analysis," and then proceed to analyze. He was equally adept at swift reversals. "On the other hand," he would say, "I can equally well imagine a situation where . . ." As he warmed up to his subject, he had a habit of cracking his knuckles and rubbing his hands together as if he were washing them.

After the milk shake at Easton's, which somehow in itself made me feel better about infinity, Willie took me for a walk down Main Street to Court Hill, striding along briskly and analyzing fluently. "There are many infinities," he announced. "Take the matter of the Name, which bothers you so much. Personally, I'm an agnostic, but I can well imagine a situation where at the very heart of things there is a simple, cosmic, unifying truth. This is the Name. Or if you prefer," he added magnanimously, "God. *Everything* is an infinity. Take that fellow Kelly, who threw the steel bolt out the window at Mr. Reilly. I will go so far as to say that if you thoroughly analyzed Kelly's motives, you would stub your toe on another infinity—the infinity of responsibility."

In my father's rather melancholy conversation, there was a good deal about blood, and especially about the shedding of what he invariably referred to specifically as "Jewish blood." I knew from early on that Jewish blood had always flowed copiously, but I had never been much affected by this knowledge.

My father's preoccupation with the subject bored me; it seemed like a peevish dwelling on old grievances, and I wasn't interested, because I didn't know what the grievances were. They had no actuality. But the attack on Mr. Reilly, to which Willie had referred, had suddenly dramatized my father's preoccupation. It happened one Saturday afternoon on Winter Street, in front of Lavin & Lupkin's dry-goods store, where I sometimes worked on Saturdays as an errand boy. Mr. Reilly was a nice old Irishman with a beautiful head of silver hair and a flowing white beard. He was a peddler, and he used to come into Lavin & Lupkin's each Saturday afternoon to stock up for his peregrinations of the following week. That day, as he approached the store, someone threw a steel bolt at him from a window of Crompton & Knowles, a factory that faced the Lavin & Lupkin building. I happened to be in the basement of L. & L.'s at the time, wrapping bundles with Willie. My brothers were there, too; they had dropped in to see Willie. We heard a commotion on the street and ran out to find Mr. Reilly lying on the sidewalk with blood flowing from a wound in his forehead. My oldest brother and the Messrs. Lavin and Lupkin carried Mr. Reilly inside; Willie ran to get Dr. Nightingale. The doctor came quickly and found that Mr. Reilly had suffered only a scalp wound, which he quickly stitched up. Within an hour, the victim was sitting happily in the office at the back of the store eating sandwiches, which I had been sent to get for him from the delicatessen down the street. Meantime, the neighborhood cop, a coreligionist of Mr. Reilly's, vowed that he would find the hurler of the bolt if it was the last thing he did.

The cop made good his word. Mr. Reilly's assailant proved to be a nineteen-year-old boy named Pat Kelly, of theretofore exemplary reputation. He confessed to his crime with a certain bravado, was arrested, and within a week was hauled up before Judge Utley. (Judge Utley bore the sobriquet in Worcester of "Thirty-Days Utley," because he habitually confined the punishment he meted out for minor offenses to that somewhat arbitrary period.) Willie and my brothers and I all went to the hearing, feeling very important, as witnesses, if not to the actual attack, at least to the events that followed it. The bolt thrower's defense was unexpected: he said the whole thing had been an optical illusion. He assured the Judge that he didn't know Mr. Reilly and had nothing whatever against him personally. Looking out of the factory window, he had seen him walking down the street and, because Mr. Reilly wore a long white beard, had concluded that he was Jewish, and had therefore thrown the bolt at him on general principles. The boy said this with such an air of guileless innocence—almost as if he had done a good deed without expectation of reward—that he was disarming. Had he known that his victim's name was Reilly, he said, he would have loved him dearly. I still remember Kelly's expression of utter bewilderment when Judge Utley was not instantly softened by an error so manifestly human and pardonable. Instead, the Judge rapped his desk sharply with his gavel and said, "Nine months in the penitentiary!" It was a sensational departure. The most the adherents of Mr. Reilly had hoped for was thirty days. Mr. Reilly, the cop, and my brothers exchanged warm and congratulatory glances, but I watched the criminal as he was taken away and saw an incredulous look on his face—the look of a man who had blundered into a topsy-turvy world.

The incident made a field day for Willie. He sat beside me at the hearing and noticed, as I did, the boy's expression of bewilderment. "I venture the opinion," said Willie on the way home, "that if you analyzed this Kelly's heredity and environment and the influences that have played on him from the time he was born, you would find that *they* threw the bolt—not Kelly!" Enlarging upon this idea, Willie worked himself up into a lather of speculation. He made an easy transition from the Winter Street incident (of about 1905) to the War Office in Paris, France, in 1899. Only the week before, Willie had taken me to Lothrop's Opera House, where I had seen my first play. It was a melodrama called "Devil's Island," and the hero was a Captain Dreyfus. It couldn't have been a very subtle play, and yet I hadn't understood it at all. This did not keep me from being thrilled by it. There was a miraculous scene at the end of the second act where the Captain escaped from Devil's Island; you actually *saw* him getting into a boat and being rowed to a sloop waiting to transport him back to Paris. You even saw the sloop. The Captain wore a waxed mustache, and although he was sorely put upon by everybody—in an earlier scene his sword had been broken and the buttons cut off his uniform before a crowd of officers, themselves in brilliant uniforms—his mustache remained glossy and imperturbable. I had never seen such aplomb. The play had a villain called Major Esterhazy, who was discomfited in the end, whereas Captain Dreyfus got his sword and his uniform back and everybody loved him. Esterhazy's discomfiture had made me happy, but now when Willie brought the bolt thrower from Crompton & Knowles and the villain of "Devil's Island" close together in a wonderful juxtaposition, I wasn't so sure. Willie went so far as to say that if you subjected Major Esterhazy to the same patient analysis he was prepared to give Pat Kelly, you would discover that outside, stronger forces, not Esterhazy, had wrought the evil against Captain Dreyfus. Ultimately, Esterhazy was innocent. Ultimately, the bolt thrower from Crompton & Knowles was innocent. To Willie, they were both nice fellows who had been badly used by their heredities and environments.

Some years earlier, Willie had had a far harder time absolving me of guilt. I was quite a small boy then, and for weeks I suffered an anguish of remorse over my inexplicable cruelty to a cat of which I was fond. I had made friends with the cat—a yellow-furred, blue-eyed vagrant—and when I walked down Providence Street, he would follow me. Flattered by his fidelity, I sometimes lifted him up and carried him, and he seemed to enjoy that. He especially liked to accompany me on my hunts for odds and ends in the dump yard that was next to the Crompton & Knowles factory. The yard was a fascinating place, containing all sorts of oddments—zinc shavings, acid jars, heavy rubber bands that had fastened the covers of the jars, flat pieces of metal, oddly stamped. It was particularly rich in tinfoil, which we boys used to collect, roll up into balls, and send off somewhere for the few pennies it would bring us. The yard was iridescent with coal dust and the vivid discoloration of decay. On very hot days, the dust gave off a heat of its own and the rubber bands bubbled. The cat seemed to enjoy prowling about the yard as much as I did, though there could have been small nourishment in it for him. One hot summer day, after taking a rich bag, my pockets bulging with baking bits of glass and metal and rubber, I started home to sort out my treasures in the privacy of our back yard. The cat trotted happily beside me. Perhaps to compensate him for having found so little for himself when I had so much, I picked him up and carried him. It was terribly hot and the loot in my pockets burned against me. I began to feel a miserable discomfort, and the climb up Providence Street seemed insupportable. I stopped for a moment, grasped the cat firmly, and threw him head first onto the sidewalk. I heard his skull crack. The sound unnerved me so much that I could not bear to look down at the cat. I went on up the hill. The stuff in my pockets now felt heavy as well as hot and I began throwing it away. By the time I got home, I had nothing left. I kept hearing the sound of the cat's skull hitting the sidewalk. In the yard next to ours, there were some cherry trees, and that day the cherries were ripe and glowed in the sun. I climbed one of the trees, though it was forbidden, and picked a few cherries. When I got down to the ground, I threw them away and ran back to find the cat. I knew exactly where I had hurled him down; it was in front of Cassie MacMahon's house. When I reached the spot, the cat was gone. I never saw him again.

Willie had a hard time with me about the cat. For a long time, I wouldn't tell him what was wrong, but he knew that something was bothering me and he finally got it out of me. He called on his standbys, heredity and environment, to assist him in absolving me, but they didn't work as well as they did, later, for Kelly and Esterhazy, whose heredities and environments Willie did not know. Unfortunately, he knew all about mine.

My father and mother were both gentle people. My father, who was almost perpetually in mourning for ancient bloodletting, had an abhorrence of violence of all sorts. I implored Willie never, never to tell my father about the cat; his anger and humiliation would have been terrible. Somewhat in a corner, Willie turned from my parents, whom we knew, to their ancestors, whom we did not know. Among them, Willie hinted as tactfully as he could, there might have been an aberrant murderer. It was unlikely, but it was possible. Or perhaps I had done this cruel thing only out of curiosity, to see what would happen. If this was so, Willie said, it had been a purely scientific impulse. He kept telling me to put the incident out of my mind and stop worrying about it. But I did worry about it, because it revealed such unaccountable and dreadful potentialities within me. I kept hearing the sharp sound of the cat's skull on the brick sidewalk. I hear it still, after more than fifty years.

The most precious possession in our Providence Street tenement was my father's many-volumed edition of the Talmud. The books were great tomes bound in calf, with marbled covers. My father had inherited them from his father and had brought them with him from Europe. I grew up with these books and saw them constantly, but since they were written in Hebrew, I was never able to read them, for though I studied Hebrew briefly when I was quite a small boy, I never got sufficiently proficient to read or understand the esoteric complexities of the Talmud. I used to stare at the pages, wondering what fascinating secrets they contained. I remember the look of those pages—grave, wide, solid columns of text in the center and, islanding them, equally solid columns of finer print. This finer print, my father explained to me, was the Rashi, or commentary on the text. Did it contain dissenting opinions, or what? I never knew.

My father and his comrades-in-learning made it their goal to go through one of the volumes of the Talmud, text and commentary, annually. The group met once a month, in the afternoon, at the homes of the different members. I remember how my mother, on the one day of the year when it was my father's turn to play host, would sit in the kitchen, her own preparations made, waiting for the summons and hoping that some perfectionist was not being too difficult over the minutiae of interpretation. The tea and cakes and liquor could not be served and the festivities begin until the last page of the day's stint had been reached. The scholars sat in the dining room—the only time in the year, except for Passover, when it was used. Normally we ate in the kitchen; using the dining room was like opening the throne room of a palace. When the food was finally served, I was allowed in and given a piece of cake— I suppose as an encouragement to emulate my elders—but it was sometimes hours before I got this unearned reward. I used to peep in, but I would be shooed away until the last moot point had been settled. I remember, on one of these occasions, conceiving a strong dislike for the father of one of my playmates, because he was pedantic and kept raising questions. I still see the Rembrandtesque scene: The men sat around the table, the great books before them; it was late afternoon and the tension was so great that no one had bothered to turn on the lamp; the heckler was insistent; Rabbi Silver pushed his glasses back on his forehead and pondered; no one moved and the silence was intense; all eyes were fixed on Rabbi Silver, imploring resolution of this crisis of interpretation. It came. Rabbi Silver readjusted his glasses and spoke. Everyone was satisfied, even the heckler. The relief was tremendous. The books were closed and the scholars relaxed in their chairs, jolly and suddenly garrulous. My father nodded to me to tell my mother that the refreshments could be brought in. After that, it was all fun.

With some of my pals whose flats were furnished, as ours was, with many-volumed editions of the Talmud, I speculated on the contents of these mysterious books. We were like those medieval inquirers who theorized in a vacuum, without ever consulting nature. Since we could none of us read the text, there was really no other way to go about it.

But scraps and fragments came to us from older boys, sons of the pundits for whom Talmud reading was a full-time occupation. These older boys were often satirical; it seemed to me they were even blasphemous. The books, they said, were not mysterious at all but discussed quite practical problems—what to do and how to behave in critical emergencies. For example, two men are walking along the street, coming from opposite directions. Simultaneously, they spy on the ground a valuable object. Each one makes for it. One says, "This find is mine!" The other makes an equally valid claim. What to do, since the object is indivisible? One scoffer used to insist that the problems discussed in the Talmud were remote and had little to do with everyday life in Worcester. He swore that one of the Talmudic situations pondered by our parents was this: A man is walking on a rampart; at the foot of the rampart an unmarried girl is taking the air; the man on the rampart slips and falls; regrettably, he falls on the girl, and she becomes pregnant. What, then, is the status of this fortuitous pregnancy? This particular skeptic felt that it was unprofitable to spend so much time on a problem so remote from Providence Street, where there were no ramparts. Whether this situation is actually discussed in the Talmud, I don't know, but I certainly grew up believing that the holy book was full of tidbits like that.

Still, generally speaking, I was tolerant, and even

a little proud, of our Talmud—perhaps because, on the hill, my father's authority on it set him up as a sage and a scholar—and I liked to leaf through the volumes. The one in which my father had written our birth dates continued to bother me. They forced me to think unhappily about what was, apparently, an immense discrepancy between my present environment and my antecedents. There were no family portraits in the house, no evidence of any direct ancestors. The only portraits on our walls were engravings of Jewish saints who had lived in the Middle Ages. These appeared to be all the progenitors we had, and they weren't even relations. We seemed to have come right out of the Middle Ages. To be sure, we had one living grandmother, my mother's mother, who sat in a rocking chair in my aunt's flat, radiating affection, but before her day was a great anterior darkness. I asked my parents questions about their pasts but could find out very little. All I knew was that my father had embarked for America at Hamburg, with my mother and the two elder children, in the steerage of a boat that was headed for New York. Apparently what had troubled him most on this journey was the fear that he would be unable to observe the dietary laws. He had come to Worcester because my uncle was there. I asked this uncle why *he* had come, and he said because he had a cousin in Boston.

But if there was little talk about the family past, there was incessant talk about pogroms. I was bored with these pogroms. When the Kishinev Massacre occurred, in April, 1903, it was a kind of windfall for my father. He had sensed my apathy about sharing his indignation and his grief over the earlier pogroms, and now, with a certain sorrowful triumph, he pointed to the newspaper headlines on Kishinev and said, "That, my son, is a pogrom!" It had happened not far from his original home. But even then what struck me as grotesque was that my father, who had made a journey to escape a peril as formidable as this, could still have been worried about dietary laws. It seemed to me to show no sense of proportion. I felt myself drifting away from him.

Increasingly, I felt the weight on me of bygone blood feuds, of oppression from dead centuries. This malaise, too, I confided to Willie. He met it with gusto. It was a natural for him. He gave me an alluring invitation. "Take Kishinev," he said. I was inclined to refuse it, but he insisted. Willie was widely, if vagariously, read, and right after offering me Kishinev he offered me Saint Bartholomew's Day, of which I had not previously heard. "Part of the pattern of history," said Willie, with a large wave of the hand. "Kishinev is only a Saint Bartholomew's Day reserved for Jews!" He made it seem that there was a certain distinction in it. My complaint about the absence of family portraits and the obscurity of my antecedents he met with a disquisition on the mystery and infinity of the chain of birth. When I pointed out that my birth date was recorded in an incomprehensible language and by a vanished calendar, he was withering. "You were *born*, weren't you?" he demanded, making it seem like an incredible feat. According to Willie, it actually was an incredible feat. "I will go as far as to say," he went on rapturously, "that the simple statement you may read anywhere on any tombstone, 'Born 1888,' say—born anywhere, any time—is the most dramatic of all declarations. Think of the nexus behind it." Nexus was a word of which Willie was very fond. "Think of the nexus of dangers and the collusion of circumstances that have to be just right before you can say of anybody that he was born. Think of the accidents you have to escape, the menaces from man and from nature! In each individual, once he manages to be born, there is a majesty of ancestry that reaches back to the very beginnings of time. Let's say you did have family portraits. How far back could they go? If you had enough of them, you couldn't give them houseroom. You'd have to have a warehouse!" Willie managed to make me feel that to wish to have ancestral portraits was to be unbearably spoiled and snobbish and extravagant.

I began to have an odd feeling that Willie, much as I adored him, was himself a kind of medievalist, and I had a longing to escape from him also. It was an extension, with contemporary references, to what I got at home. I began to weary of his "patterns of history" and to see that he only added to the infinities to which I had been introduced by my father. You could scarcely bring up anything with Willie without being caught up in a nexus. I longed for something without an attendant nexus.

I found it in the Worcester Public Library. I found it specifically in the Alger books. The library had an enormous number of them and I devoured them; I used to take out one a day, swallow it, and return it the next day for another. They were heaven. The heroes had limited and attainable objectives and they always made them. I was astonished to discover that not one of them was worried about the Name or about infinity; they just wanted to make money. They were not materialists merely; they wanted to be good as well as to succeed. But goodness was defined and success was defined: they were like targets in a well-lighted shooting gallery. If your nervous system was not undermined by drink or vice, if you were virtuous, your aim would be true and the target vulnerable. The characters took their births for granted, their lives for granted; even the bad ones, even the villains, were not ashamed of their villainy; they had a free right to it. And they all lived and breathed in a zippy and exhilarating climate—the climate of America, the climate of Worcester itself on an October day. Somehow the escapes offered by Willie were almost as stifling as the dilemmas they explained: they were corridors from nexus to nexus. They were exonerations. The Alger heroes were really free. When they were unhappy, when things looked dark for them, when evil appeared momentarily to have the upper hand, they were still exhilaratingly and miraculously free. And they came through; they demonstrated that you could succeed in life without worrying about infinity. If any of them had any suspicion that the current names of the Lord were merely stop-gaps and that the True Name was wrapped in tantalizing mystery, they gave no evidence of it. Phil the Fiddler, Jed the Poor House Boy, Ragged Dick, Tom the Bootblack had plenty of handicaps, but these were all tangible, exterior, present, visible. They were not dragged down by the past; they had only to penetrate the future. The future was not bent back into infinity; it was like a wide and navigable river, explorable. The hero of "From Canal Boy to President" made it without a single nexus in his meagre luggage; what he carried in his carpetbag was utilitarian.

Willie's penchant for separating problems into their component parts got full play while I was in high school. He helped me in the inter-high-school debates and he gave me a major position on a little staff of researchers he organized, whose object was to win the large sums of money offered by the Boston papers at that time in their puzzle contests.

Willie was a great believer in hobbies, and for a period the solution of these puzzles became his major hobby and an extracurricular activity for me. There were, I remember, a Proverb Contest, a Great Names Contest, and a Familiar Sayings Contest, among others, and the prizes offered by the *Herald, Globe,* or *Post* in their circulation drives were bigger, actually, than those offered nowadays by the radio and television Santa Clauses and far more satisfactory, since instead of winning pressure cookers, and deep freezes full of hams, you could win thousand-dollar and hundred-dollar and fifty-dollar bills.

Willie approached these contests scientifically, mobilizing all his resources to take them out of the hit-or-miss area of gambling and transmute them into a rational pursuit. I remember particularly our exhaustive researches for the Familiar Sayings Contest. Every day, there appeared in one of the papers—which one I now forget—an untitled drawing illustrating some saying, and you were supposed to supply five aphorisms, in the order of your preference, as your five captions for each picture. If you hit the right saying on your fourth choice and somebody else had hit it on his first, you naturally lost out. The final winner, after several weeks of daily effort, was to be the person who had the highest percentage of early guesses. Willie's surveys of previous contests had shown that the "mass average" of the winners was what counted most heavily; that is to say, the winners were not usually those

257

who had the most firsts but those who had the greatest number of correct answers among their first three choices. Willie put in a lot of heavy reading on the laws of probability and averages, and we were soon moving in the high realm of numerical theory. We were equipped in every way: we kept elaborate card-catalogue files; we reduced the element of chance to a minimum; we were scientifically and theoretically right. But we didn't win that contest—or any other.

It was during my junior and senior years in high school that Willie encouraged me to take part, under his tutelage, in the inter-high-school debates. Here his special dialectic method—his "On the other hand I can imagine"s and "I venture the opinion"s—served him admirably, and, thanks to his coaching, I became the president of the Sumner Club, Classical High's debating society. If, for instance, the Sumner Club took the affirmative in a debate on the referendum and recall, or on whether capital punishment should be abolished, Willie would bone up on the negative, in order to prime me with answers to any points our opponents might raise. He and I used to work for hours together in the Public Library reading room, handing Poole's Index back and forth between us. Willie attended all the debates, and if the Sumner Club team won, Willie always came up to congratulate me, beaming as happily as Diaghilev might have done after a triumph of Nijinsky's.

It was because of Willie, as I have said, that my family decided to send me to Clark College instead of to work. Willie used to follow my progress in English under Dr. Loring Dodd, reading the themes I wrote for him and judiciously cogitating the professor's marginal comments. When Dr. Dodd gave me a bad mark on a theme, Willie took it hard. Though Dr. Dodd did not know it, Willie was his unofficial assistant.

After I had been at Clark for two years, Willie began to read about George Pierce Baker and his new Drama Workshop at Harvard, which was then much in the news. I had started writing short stories, and Willie labored over them painfully, spending a long time placing commas; he was fascinated by commas and would go into a dithyramb on their loveliness. But since all my stories were swiftly rejected by the magazines Willie and I submitted them to, he thought maybe I should turn to the drama. Once the idea hit him, nothing would serve but my going to Harvard to study under Professor Baker. The transfer from Clark was difficult, but Willie arranged it and I moved to Cambridge for my junior and senior years. Our relations continued close. Willie was delighted when, after submitting an essay to Charles Townsend Copeland, I received a postcard from Copey admitting me to English 12, and he was positively triumphant when, in my senior year, after submitting a one-act play to George Pierce Baker, I was invited to join English 47, the playwriting course Willie had read so much about in the newspapers.

By then, Willie had married and was practicing law in Worcester. His wife, whom I knew well, since she grew up on Providence Street, was devoted to him, and she accepted his friendship for me with tolerance, as she accepted his other idiosyncrasies. Willie came often to Cambridge to see me, and during my holidays in Worcester I had high times and rampant discussions with him. We gave commas and theories of all sorts a brisk workout. However, during the summer between my junior and senior years at Harvard—the last months I was to spend in Worcester—I became aware, without being able exactly to put my finger on it, of some cloud that occasionally shadowed Willie's usual exuberance. For one thing, he was worrying about his inability to concentrate. He had theories about concentration, and, by the standard of what he called "ultimate concentration," he found himself woefully lacking. I pointed out to him that he seemed able to pass with ease the most difficult examinations, which certainly must mean that he could concentrate. Perhaps, although I was too young to realize it then, he had begun to worry about his inability to concentrate on anything except the abstract, and to realize that when he was faced with the workaday problems of practicing a profession, he shied off. One day in the fall of my senior year, he startled me by calling me on the telephone to ask if I could make an appointment for him in Boston with a reliable psychiatrist. I inquired around and was given the name of a well-known doctor, and made an appointment with him for Willie. I went with Willie to the doctor's office, and sat in the waiting room during the consultation. I could never find out much about what took place, but I gathered later that Willie felt the famous psychiatrist's views on his special problem were "superficial." Willie quit him after that one visit but went several times to see another Boston psychiatrist. Before long, he began to pull out of this particular depression and told me with a laugh that he'd found he couldn't even concentrate on a psychiatrist.

By the time of my graduation in June, a ceremony that Willie attended, he was his old self again. After that, I went to New York to live with my brothers, who were already established there in their own accounting firm, but I kept in constant touch with Willie by letter and phone, and we met during my frequent visits to Worcester to see my mother. My brothers were expert accountants, and perhaps it was their influence that made Willie suddenly determine to switch careers again. He had decided that accounting was a fresh field in Worcester and that his legal training would be a help in it, so he once more studied in Boston, and, at the end of his course, passed the difficult examination that qualified him as a certified public accountant.

Meanwhile, I was having a tough time in New York. As I was unable to get a job, I did graduate work at Columbia. After I had received my M.A. degree, I got an offer of an instructorship at the University of Minnesota, at twelve hundred dollars a year. I accepted it. Just as I was about to leave for the West, Willie made one of his visits to New York to see my brothers and me. He went first to see my brothers at their office, where they told him about my appointment. Willie took a poor view of it. In fact, he put his foot down. I must stay in New York and go on writing, he told them. It was extraordinary how firm and decisive Willie could be about any problem affecting *me*. Nevertheless, my oldest brother and I started out the next day to buy a round-trip ticket to Minneapolis, but when we discovered that the fare would use almost half of my first year's salary, we gave up the idea. Willie was delighted when he heard this; he rubbed his palms together and cracked his knuckles with elation.

In 1926, I sold my first play. Within an hour after I heard that it had been accepted for production, I was on the train to Worcester to tell Willie about it. No telephone call would serve for such great news. He came to the opening night in New York, and instead of going to the party given for the cast, I met him in Childs after the play. Willie was in fine fettle. He elaborated on the difference between the drama and other literary forms. I had, he decided, made a good choice, and I reflected, without saying so, that it was Willie's choice as much as mine.

Then I began to travel a bit, but before every journey I would telephone Willie in Worcester, and I always called him up within an hour of my return. We also kept up an incessant correspondence. At the end of one long absence from New York, I asked my brothers for a report on Willie. They said that they were worried about him, and told me that one day while they were walking with him and discussing accounting problems, Willie had stopped in the street to point out an advertising sign and ask them whether they could explain the mystery of a conjunction in the sign. Why was it there? One of my brothers said that it was just a connective word. Willie wouldn't let it go at that. He said he was increasingly troubled by the function of conjunctions, prepositions, and relative clauses in sentences. After a bit, he let it go and was his usual jolly self.

When my brothers told me this, I had that tantalizing sense of recurrence that so often afflicts one. Out of a drowse of memory, out of a very distant past, I heard again (did I remember it or didn't I?) a long wrangle between Willie and my father while I lay in my bedroom on Providence Street, supposed to be asleep but actually wide-awake and eavesdropping. I heard my father talking to Willie as he had to me, setting limits to certain fields of inquiry, and Willie valiantly rejecting any limits, which I had never had the courage to do. I began to remember more clearly: My father had said you mustn't, for example, speculate overmuch on infinity. I wondered whether Willie was now continuing his early defiance of my father. Had he merely shifted the focus from the cosmic to the infinitesimal, both illimitable? Was Willie suffocating from some constriction of curiosity that he couldn't work out of? In his arguments with my father, Willie had flouted mystery in favor of illumination. Was Willie now lost in mystery? Had my father been right to set limits and Willie wrong to ignore my father's "Keep Off" signs? For the first time since I had known Willie, I began to feel a deep malaise about him. Before long, I shook it off, telling myself that, after all, this was merely another manifestation of his lifelong fetish for analyzing things and breaking them down into their component parts.

In one's later middle life, long journeys become perilous, because of the workings of mortality at home. To return and find that somebody one has dearly loved has died in one's absence gives one a sense of special loss, almost a feeling of having been callous, as if by not being present one had failed to prevent or delay the loss. I had this strange feeling after my mother died while I was on the way back from a trip to Europe; almost the same thing happened to me, years earlier and under the same circumstances, with Willie. In Willie's case, my sense of having deserted was particularly poignant, because his death was what is referred to glibly and superficially as "voluntary." In the summer of 1928, I was sailing from New York for Europe, and I had a long-distance telephone talk with Willie just before I boarded the ship. By that time, he was in his fourth career. Willie's father had sold his retail store to go into manufacturing, and Willie had abandoned accounting to serve as an executive in his father's factory. When I talked with him the evening I sailed, he was gay, and told me proud anecdotes about his two children. I was going to be very busy and would be moving about a good deal in Europe on that trip, with many changes of address, so we agreed not to write to each other while I was away.

Several months later, on my return, one of my brothers met me at the pier, as he did later when my mother died, and took me to my hotel. I went at once to the telephone to put in a call to Willie, but my brother stopped me. He told me that Willie was dead. He said that a few months earlier Willie had had some kind of nervous breakdown and had been sent to a neurological institution in Massachusetts, where it was confidently expected that he could be cured. He had seemed to be getting better and only a few weeks before my return he had had a cheerful visit at the hospital with his wife and children. The evening after that visit, he had broken the window of his room and cut his throat with a piece of glass.

Along with my grief, I felt a kind of terrible self-reproach; I could not repress the feeling that if I had been there, I might, by some miracle of friendship, have held off the steep, dark walls that converged on Willie to extinguish him. The residual medieval superstition that those who are afflicted by mental illness are possessed by devils dies hard. I have seen people who are sincerely sympathetic in cases of physical illness behave toward people suffering from mental diseases as though they were self-indulgent, capricious, or perverse. For one thing, those so bedevilled (the very word is a legacy of the superstition!) are often at large, stumbling through the ordinary thickets of social life, where, unprotected by the accoutrements of the sickroom, they have to endure criticism instead of being comforted by compassion. And yet their sort of mental suffering impinges on the most delicate and mysterious and impenetrable of our faculties—the faculty that is the source of idiosyncrasy, of the distinguishing trait, of what differentiates us from the inarticulate animals and from each other. Where the mind is touched, the taut string at the heart of the personality is plucked. If one could trace to its source that wild logic that compels those like Willie to their deaths, one would have solved the mystery of one of the infinities in which we swim.

I have asked many psychiatrists about Willie, and all of them have told me that he was probably a "schizophrenic." This is a cataloguing and descriptive word. What does it explain of the mystery that goes on within the human mind? The psychiatrists have also told me that autopsies in such cases reveal no lesion in the brain. It is perhaps an evidence of the persistence of the magic and mystery in my inheritance that in my rebellious and passionate grieving at finding myself in a world without Willie I recalled the talk I had had with him when I was a child and was troubled about the enigma of the Name. Willie had been well able to understand my tribulation then, and he had ventured the opinion to me, as I had to my father, that someday, somewhere, there would emerge an intelligence subtle enough and courageous enough to hear the true name of the Lord, even if it destroyed him. Had Willie, in his lonely hours, importunately sought the Name? Had he, I wondered, come too close?

ABOUT THE AUTHOR

Samuel Nathaniel Behrman (1893-1973), the son of Jewish Lithuanian immigrants, was born in Worcester, Massachusetts and grew up in a triple-decker at #31 Providence Street. His father was a grocer and a Talmudic scholar who taught Hebrew to neighborhood children. In Worcester, Behrman attended Providence Street School, Classical High School, and Clark University. He transferred to Harvard University after two years at Clark and enrolled in Harvard's famous "47 Workshop" for drama students. After graduation in 1916, he went to New York and earned a masters degree from Columbia University before pursuing a writing career. He eventually authored 20 plays, 6 books, 21 movie scripts and countless periodical articles.

The Worcester Account was first published by Random House in 1954 as a compilation of pieces which had previously appeared in the *New Yorker* magazine. This book is a collection of his memoirs from early childhood through adulthood. "The Cold Wind and the Warm," a play based on *The Worcester Account*, was produced in New York in 1958 starring Maureen Stapleton and Eli Wallach, and featuring newcomer Suzanne Pleshette.

Behrman continued a second phase in his interesting career with the publication of *The Worcester Account*. This phase consisted of prose works (as opposed to plays); among them are *Duveen* (1952), *Portrait of Max* (1960), and *People in a Diary* (1972). *Duveen,* the story of a phenomenal art dealer who convinced American millionaires that they needed to buy European masterpieces, has been republished several times since it first appeared and has been translated into several foreign languages. A Japanese edition was published in 1990.

Behrman's first hit Broadway play, "The Second Man," produced in 1927, established his reputation as a playwright and led to many writing offers in Hollywood. He began writing snappy dialogue for the new talking pictures during the Depression. Many of his screenplays became renowned adaptations of classic plays and novels: *Daddy Long Legs* (1931), *Rebecca of Sunnybrook Farm* (1932), *Queen Christina* (1933), *The Scarlet Pimpernel* (1934), *Anna Karenina* (1935), *Waterloo Bridge* (1940), *Quo Vadis* (1951). His critically acclaimed 1934 play, "Rain From Heaven," was the first American play to draw attention to the horrors of the Nazi regime and to the impact it was having on the Jewish population.

Behrman wrote for Hollywood's best and brightest, including Greta Garbo, Al Jolson, Basil Rathbone, Charles Boyer, Clark Gable, Leslie Howard, Raymond Massie, Vivien Leigh, Gary Cooper, Myrna Loy, Merle Oberon, Deborah Kerr, Danny Kaye, and Peter Ustinov. Throughout his career, he continued writing original works and never lost his social conscience.

Works by S. N. Behrman

Books

Duveen, 1952
The Worcester Account, 1954
*Portrait of Max: An Intimate Memoir of Sir Max
 Beerbohm,* 1960
The Suspended Drawing Room, 1965
The Burning Glass, 1968
People in a Diary: A Memoir, 1972

Plays

The Second Man, 1927
Love Is Like That, 1927
Serena Blandish; or the Difficulty of Getting Married, 1929
Meteor, 1929
Brief Moment, 1931
Biography, 1932
Love Story, 1933
Rain From Heaven, 1934
End of Summer, 1936
Amphitryon 38, 1937 (adapted from the French of Giraudoux)
Wine of Choice, 1938
No Time for Comedy, 1939
The Talley Method, 1941
The Pirate, 1942 (from Fulda)
Jacobowsky and the Colonel, 1944 (with Franz Werfel)
Dunnigan's Daughter, 1945
I Know My Love, 1949
Let Me Hear the Melody, 1951
Jane, 1952 (from Somerset Maugham)
Fanny, 1954 (with Joshua Logan)
The Cold Wind and the Warm, 1958
Lord Pengo, 1962
But for Whom Charlie, 1964

Works by S. N. Behrman

Movie Screenplays

Liliom, 1930
Sea Wolf, 1930
Lightnin', 1930
Daddy Long Legs, 1931
Surrender, 1931
Rebecca of Sunnybrook Farm, 1932
Tess of the Storm Country, 1932
My Lips Betray, 1933
As Husbands Go, 1933
Hallelujah, I'm a Bum!, 1933
Queen Christina, 1933
The Scarlet Pimpernel, 1934
Anna Karenina, 1935
A Tale of Two Cities, 1935
Parnell, 1937
Conquest, 1937
The Cowboy and the Lady, 1938
Waterloo Bridge, 1940
Two-Faced Woman, 1941
Quo Vadis, 1951
Me and the Colonel, 1958

spoke ...

"Where have you been ...
"With the boys. Play ...
"Go to sleep. Say ...
I went into the be...
Hebrew prayer undressing ...
on a flow of wakeful dream...
around, free, under the deep
pursued, to feel danger. Ho...
when I was grown up the ...
which I would so!
My father's heavy
thoughts. He was pacing up
solemnity his Hebrew pray...
at my head thy hand. I sa...
Michael? For the matter of ...
fathers so eternally preoccup...
so painfully on a night lik...
stay home — praying —
books — no matter how ...
even as I relaps...
the slow step and the u...